NO LONGER PROPERTY OF
ANYTHINK LIBRARIES/
RANGEVIEW LIBRARY DISTRICT

They Came to the Manger

They Came to the Manger

to the

Manger

Heartwarming Christmas Tales
of Creatures Great and Small

Guideposts
New York, New York

They Came to the Manger

ISBN-13: 978-0-8249-4819-1

Published by Guideposts
16 East 34th Street
New York, New York 10016
www.guideposts.com

Copyright © 2010 by Guideposts. All rights reserved.

This book, or parts thereof, may not be reproduced, stored in a retrieval system, or transmitted in any form or by any means, electronic, mechanical, photocopying, recording or otherwise, without the written permission of the publisher.

Distributed by Ideals Publications, a Guideposts company
2630 Elm Hill Pike, Suite 100
Nashville, Tennessee 37214

Guideposts and *Ideals* are registered trademarks of Guideposts.

Acknowledgments

Every attempt has been made to credit the sources of copyrighted material used in this book. If any such acknowledgment has been inadvertently omitted or miscredited, receipt of such information would be appreciated.

"The Land between the Rivers" by Arthur Gordon is from *Through Many Windows* by Arthur Gordon. Copyright © 1985 by Arthur Gordon. Published by Fleming H. Revell. Used by permission.

"The Christmas Day Kitten" by James Herriot is copyright © 1976, 1986 by James Herriot. Reprinted by permission of David Higham Associates Ltd. and St. Martin's Press.

"Bill's Christmas Miracle" by Bill Edwards is from *The Blessing of the Animals* by Philip Gonzalez. Copyright © 1996 by Philip Gonzalez and Leonore Fleischer. Reprinted by permission of HarperCollins Publishers.

"The Christmas Visit" by Jo Coudert is copyright © 1998 by Jo Coudert. Reprinted by permission of the Richard Parks Agency.

"Luther" by Michelle Wheeler Culmore is reprinted from *Christmas in My Heart*, volume 4, compiled and edited by Joe L. Wheeler. Copyright © 1995 by Review and Herald Publishing Association. Reprinted by permission of Joe L. Wheeler.

"A Parrot Taught Me Her Song" by Ronald L. Harmon and "Saved by Dolphins" by Anne Archer are from *Angel Animals*, copyright © 1999, 2007 by Allen and Linda Anderson. Reprinted with permission of New World Library, Novato, CA. www.newworldlibrary.com

"The Undersea Reindeer" by Allan Zullo is from *The Dog Who Saved Christmas and Other True Animal Tales* by Allan Zullo. Copyright © 2008 by the Wordsellers, Inc. Reprinted by permission of Scholastic Inc.

"Christmas" by Eric Swanson is reprinted from *Hero Cats* by Eric Swanson. Copyright © 1998. Reprinted by permission of Andrews McMeel Universal, Kansas City, MO.

"Igabella, the Perfect Present" by Mary Alice Baumgardner, "The Gift of Lucy" by Lonnie Hull Dupont, "A Doggie Kind of Christmas" by Nancy Tomazic, "A Christmas Miracle" by Crystal Ward Kent, "Catfish Promises" by Anne Culbreath Watkins, "Sometimes Angels Come in Disguise" by Renie Szilak Burghardt are reprinted by permission of the authors.

Our sincere thanks for the poetry of Alice Leedy Mason and "Kitten of Bethlehem" by Ruth C. Ikerman.

All other stories are reprinted by permission of Guideposts.

Library of Congress Cataloging-in-Publication Data has been applied for.

They came to the manger : heartwarming Christmas tales of creatures great and small.
    p. cm.
ISBN 978-0-8249-4819-1
1. Domestic animals—Anecdotes.   2. Christmas—Anecdotes.   3. Christmas stories.
SF76.5.T44   2010
242'.335—dc22   2010028291

Edited and compiled by Elizabeth Kramer Gold
Cover and interior design by Thinkpen Design
Cover art by Simon Mendez
Typeset by Aptara

Printed in the United States of America
10 9 8 7 6 5 4 3 2 1

Contents

Comfort & Joy

Christmas Miracles

The Blessing of the Animals

They Came
to the
Manger

Introduction

The Nativity story starts with a man and a woman on a donkey—both on their way to the town of Bethlehem. Unable to find any accommodations, they are lodged in a stable, where, that night, Jesus is born and placed in a manger. Angels proclaim the birth to shepherds tending their flocks in nearby fields: "Glory to God in the highest, and on earth peace, good will toward men."

This transformative moment is known and loved by people around the world—it is the subject of stories, hymns, paintings, movies and countless Christmas pageants. It lives in our hearts. But there is an element present in this story that we don't always consider: the donkey Mary is riding, the animals in the stable watching this event, the sheep in the fields. Animals witness the most important moment of humankind.

This volume is a collection of Christmas animal stories. The first section consists of legends about Christmas—the donkey dealer who sold the animal who carried Mary into Bethlehem and how that animal behaved. There are stories of a kitten and a camel who witness the birth. And then there is another donkey—the one who will carry mother and child safely into Egypt.

And the rest of the volume—true stories of animals at Christmas! These animals comfort us, surprise us and make us laugh. They remind us that God's love comes in many forms. There are the stories one would expect: the Christmas puppy, the kitten that plays among the wrapping paper. But most surprising is the diversity of God's creatures: the Christmas iguana, the goose who escaped from the table, birds whose songs cheer us.

There are stories of rescue: a horse who saves soldiers on Christmas day, dolphins who help a swimmer find her way back to shore, a deer that points the way home.

Each one of these stories is witness to the miracle of God's world and of his love for all his creatures. Each story reminds us how we can gain comfort and give love to each other and to the animals around us at Christmas and year-round. ❅

Legends & Fables of Christmas

Christmas Legends

DENIS A. MCCARTHY

Christmas morn, the legends say,
Even the cattle kneel to pray,
Even the beasts of wood and field
Homage to Christ the Savior yield.
Horse and cow and woolly sheep
Wake themselves from their heavy sleep,
Bending heads and knees to him
Who came to earth in a stable dim.
Faraway in the forest dark
Creatures timidly wake and hark.
Feathered bird and furry beast
Turn their eyes to the mystic east.
Loud at the dawning, chanticleer
Sounds his note, the rest of the year,
But Christmas Eve, the whole night long
Honoring Christ he sings his song.
Christmas morn, the legends say,
Even the cattle kneel to pray,
Even the wildest beast afar
Knows the light of the Savior's star.

Jared, the Donkey Dealer

DINA DONAHUE

ared, the donkey dealer, was becoming annoyed and tired. All day he had been besieged by travelers who had to make long journeys. They bargained with him, made fun of his animals and tried to cheat him. Well, he thought, no one was going to beat Jared, especially since he knew these travelers had no choice but to go.

The new decree handed down by Caesar Augustus had proclaimed that every man throughout the land must return to the city from which his family had come and place his name on a register so taxes could be paid. It was a hardship for many and especially for a young couple, Joseph and Mary, of the house of David.

They faced a journey of some eighty miles from Nazareth in Galilee to Bethlehem in Judea. Mary was soon to have a child. Still, they did not dare to disobey the order.

Jared was standing with his wife at the gate of his fenced-in yard when he saw them approach.

"I need a donkey for my wife Mary to ride on our long journey," Joseph explained. "It must be a docile creature, yet strong enough for the trip. It must be amiable so Mary will be carried with gentle care. She'll soon give birth."

"You ask a lot," snarled Jared. Then he thought awhile and said, "I have just the beast for you."

Jared went inside his yard and soon returned leading a miserable-looking donkey.

"He does not look too promising," Joseph said.

"Nonsense," Jared replied quickly. "He's just right for your wife." Jared prodded the animal with a stick, but it did not move.

Mary placed her hand behind the beast's ears and gently began stroking its head. "I'm sure he's a lovely animal," she said. The donkey moved closer to her.

Reluctantly, Joseph paid the fee and, helping Mary onto the beast, started on the journey. Jared's wife turned to him and scolded:

"How could you give them such an unruly animal? One that balks so often?"

"It's not my fault if that Joseph is so trusting," Jared countered. "I'm just being a good businessman. Joseph should have led the beast about first to find out for himself. And is it my fault if he carries no stick to prod the animal?"

"Shame on you. And that poor girl expecting a child and having to ride so far. . . . " The wife turned away. "Now I see why so many say you're a hard, mean dealer."

Jared stood for a moment, deep in thought. *You have to be tough to do business in these times, don't you?* But his wife's words stung. *What if they complained? What if they told others? Why, they could ruin your business.*

Abruptly he went back inside the yard. He selected his very best animal and tying a rope about its neck, hurried down the road. In the distance, Jared saw Joseph walking beside the donkey, holding the lead. Mary, in a flowing light blue robe, sat tall.

Jared hurried up to them and called out breathlessly, "Excuse me, I made a mistake. I just discovered that I have a much better donkey for you. There will be no extra fee. Here, Joseph, you may have it." And Jared held out the lead rope to Joseph.

"But this one is just fine; we've no complaints," said Joseph.

"He didn't try to unseat your lady? Or balk?" Jared was perplexed. Always before he had had complaints about the beast. Could this be the same animal?

"No, this is a gentle, loving donkey," the soft-voiced Mary answered, her hand stroking the animal's back.

Jared couldn't understand the glow in the young wife's face. She seemed so different from the other women who had had to make the long trip. He'd heard them complaining.

Then Jared spoke, his head bent in shame. "You don't understand. You see, I willfully gave you a donkey that was . . . was . . . " Jared looked down at the dusty road and went on, " . . . that was no good. I don't want you to be hurt."

Mary smiled, her eyes filled with understanding. "Thank you for telling us, dear sir," she spoke softly. "But we like this one, and he likes us. We will make the trip safely now."

Joseph put an arm around Jared. "Yes, it's all right now. We will be going. God be with you."

"I wish you well," Jared mumbled. Then holding on to the lead of his best animal, Jared watched as the young couple continued down the road. Somehow Jared knew the young mother would do well on the long trip. "God be with you too," he whispered.

It wasn't like Jared to be concerned with the welfare of his customers: All he'd ever cared about was that they pay the fee and return the animal in good condition. But now he didn't want to be a tough, mean donkey dealer. He'd tell his wife about it. What was it that was so special about the gentle Mary? ❄

Kitten of Bethlehem

RUTH C. IKERMAN

*K*itten was tired, lonely and hungry. If only just one person would take pity on him. Then he heard the sound of an approaching donkey.

When the innkeeper picked up a stone and tossed it at the furry tail, the kitten ran as fast as he could. He didn't stop until he reached the stable behind the inn.

Cautiously he poked his head around the corner to see if there was anyone inside who would make him move on. He was very tired and hungry. The only food he had found all day was a little milk in an indentation of a big rock where some goats had been milked.

There seemed to be lots of people coming into the town just now, with official-looking men bustling about to count them and their possessions. Kitten had played around the courtyard of the busy inn, hoping some of the strangers would stop to feed him, or at least notice him.

Now the innkeeper himself had shouted at him to get out of the way, and Kitten had barely managed to reach the stable. With his bright eyes, which could see well in the dark, he looked around to find out who was there ahead of him. Good!

Here was a cow, and sometimes a little cat could make friends with a cow. If he stayed close when the good, rich milk was being taken, there might be some for him too.

Over in the stable corner was the sturdy ox with his mate. A mother hen had gathered her chicks under her wings, and they were resting in the straw.

Silently surveying the leap it would be from the dusty ground to the warm manger straw, Kitten paused for strength, for he was weak from hunger. He took a big breath—then with a quick twist of his back feet, he took off in a broad jump and landed nimbly in the sweet-smelling hay. He treaded his bed with his front paws and then dropped his furry face in a moment of surrender and rest.

But soon he heard someone entering the stable. Could the innkeeper be hunting him? He jumped up and arched his back, making his tail twice its usual size. At least he would put up a good fight if the big dogs were turned loose on him.

Instead, Kitten saw a tired little donkey entering the stable—the same kind of patient animal that had been bringing people into the inn courtyard. Kitten let his tail return to normal size before he scampered forward to welcome the newcomer. He knew what it was to be lonely and afraid, and he wanted to offer his friendship.

The donkey looked at him out of one big eye beneath a big ear, and the kitten looked back. He said, "Welcome," the sweetest tone of meow he could manage in his hunger.

The donkey halted as the man walking beside him said, "It's all right. Here we are now, with a roof over our heads and shelter for the night."

The man was speaking to a woman seated on the donkey. Tenderly he lifted her down to the manger, and she gave a soft sigh of relief. She closed her eyes and put her head back on the pillow of straw.

Kitten had never seen such a sweet, kind face. He crept closer. His paws moved a stray piece of straw that tickled the woman's arm. She opened her eyes and saw the kitten beside her. Gently the soft hands touched his head, and he felt the fear going out of him at the touch.

Holding fast to the kitten, she reached out to the man beside the donkey and said, "Oh, see what we have found! A beautiful kitten waiting with us for our baby."

Suddenly the lonely kitten felt he was within the circle of a family. His heart pounded with the sheer joy of knowing that now he belonged to someone.

The man reached into the bag that hung from the side of the donkey and took out a little brown earthen bowl. Into it he poured milk from a skin container. He crumbled a piece of brown bread into the liquid. Then he placed it on the ground and beckoned to the kitten.

How good the bread and milk tasted! Kitten tried not to take it all in greedy gulps. Methodically he cleaned the bowl. Then he withdrew on soft feet to the corner of the stable and soon was asleep.

When Kitten opened his eyes, he thought it must be morning, but the light that streamed into the open manger was not like any sunlight he had ever seen. Yet it was not like the night, either, although there were stars overhead, the same stars under which he had traveled, weary and alone, hunting a home.

An unusual radiance streamed from the largest star of all, directly over the manger. And there lay a baby, cradled beside the woman with the understanding eyes. Nearby the man stood, the weariness erased from his face in a moment of happy triumph over discouragement.

The cow chewed her cud rhythmically, and the breath of the oxen came in deep measures of satisfaction. A white chicken clucked, and the others answered drowsily. Soon all were wide awake, for glorious music filled the stable.

It seemed to Kitten that the very light was singing. Such heavenly sounds he had never heard before. He felt he would burst if he couldn't join the hallelujahs of joy.

Kitten had never learned to sing, but he wanted to be part of the chorus. He took a deep breath and let the good air come into his tiny lungs. He began to purr in time with the song he heard. Louder swelled the chorus from on high, and Kitten echoed it with his sweet, harmonious purring.

The mother turned from looking at her child and saw again the kitten, his little ribs pressing out as he purred his lullaby for the new baby. She smiled at Kitten, and over him passed a peace such as he had never expected to find on this earth.

Thinking of the gifts people would bring for the new baby, he looked up to see a white lamb approaching ahead of a shepherd with a crook. Kitten had seen such men in the hills, and sometimes one would share his food with a wandering kitten. Now a band of shepherds approached the manger as though guided by the star. They knelt and offered the beautiful lamb as a love gift.

Watching the shepherds presenting their gift to the baby, Kitten turned away in discouragement. What gift could he bring to the baby? He remembered the gentle touch of the beautiful woman, and the kindness of the man in sharing their food. There must be something he could give in return.

Deep in his heart he said, *I do not have anything to give except myself. I will give that gladly.* He moved to the foot of the manger and climbed the rough wood to the straw. He stretched out the full length of his furry coat to let its warmth comfort the tired feet of the woman, resting with the child in her arms. She put her head back and smiled. Kitten felt his heart warmed within him. His gift had been accepted in love, even as it had been offered.

He began to purr again in gratitude. He had found the rich satisfaction and peace that come from giving of oneself. Happily he closed his eyes to sleep and to gather strength for the living of his new life, which would be forever marked by the echo of the wonderful song. ❄

The Littlest Camel

SHIRLEY CLIMO

t. Francis of Assisi taught that all the gentle creatures that shared the stable with the Christ Child could share too in the anniversary of His birth. So in many countries, it is a tradition to remember the furred and feathered members of the household at Christmas. In Scandinavia, sheaves of grain are tied atop the roof to feed the hungry birds. In Spain, extra rations are given the cattle in remembrance of the cow who warmed the baby Jesus with its breath. In Belgium, and in parts of France, lambs are brought to the church to be blessed on Christmas Eve.

According to Syrian legend, one animal present at the first Christmas was blessed in a special way. The three wise men had traveled many arduous miles upon their camels before they reached the stable. When, at last the Magi dismounted to give the Christ Child their gifts, the first two camels also knelt and bowed their heads before him. But the third camel, young and wearied from so long a journey, stumbled and sprawled beside the manger. The onlookers were horrified and might have beaten the beast had not the Christ Child stayed them, lifting his small hand. He blessed the little camel and promised that henceforth it should be the bearer of gifts to all children in his name.

That is why children in Syria leave bundles of hay outside their doors on Three Kings Day (January 6). It is their thank you to "the Camel of Jesus," who, they believe, is still faithfully traveling the long miles to bring their Christmas gifts. ❄

The Land between the Rivers

ARTHUR GORDON

*L*ong ago, when the rivers of America were still silver, two of them flowed—not far apart—into the great sea. Later they would be called the Ogeechee and the Altamaha, but in those days they were nameless because there was no one to name them. No men, no women. Just the animals and birds, the trees and shrubs, and of course the wind, which was fickle and fey, but also very wise.

One cold gray twilight when the days were short, the wind spoke to the animals and the birds that lived in the land between the rivers, and to the trees and the shrubs.

"Tonight," the wind whispered, "you must stay awake, and watch, and wait, because a great happening may come upon you. What or where it will be I cannot say, because I am only the wind. But there will be a sign; this I know. And when you see it, you should rejoice and be thankful, because after this night, nothing will be the same. Stay awake, then, and be ready."

The wind sighed away into the great live oaks and across the amber marshes, and the twilight deepened, and the stars came out. The animals and the birds and the trees and the shrubs took counsel together. Most of them were doubtful, some downright scornful.

"Who can believe what is whispered by the wind?" they said. And one by one they fell asleep, the deer and the foxes, the squirrels and the shaggy bears in the swamps. Even night wanderers like the raccoons and the opossums sought their dens. The voices of the birds were stilled. They closed their bright eyes and slept. All except one small brown bird who was troubled in his heart.

"Someone must stay awake," he said to himself, "and be ready to rejoice and give thanks if this marvel does come to pass. I will wait and watch." He sought a bush or tree to perch in, but none of them wanted him.

"We have your kind all day," they grumbled. "We need our rest at night."

But one tall green shrub took pity on the bird. "Here," it said, "I don't mind. Perch on one of my branches, and I'll stay awake and watch with you." So the forest slept, and everything in it except the small brown bird perched in the tall bush, waiting.

And near midnight suddenly a golden light appeared in the sky, like a mighty star, only much bigger, much brighter. Silently it moved across the astonished heavens, and the bird and the bush watched it until it disappeared over the rim of the world.

"Ah," they said to each other, "did you see that? How wonderful it was! We really should rejoice." So the bird sang and the bush rustled its glossy leaves, and they gave thanks and praise in this fashion until the stars turned pale and the sun rose out of the sea.

Then all the creatures in the forest were amazed, because everywhere among the branches of the tall bush were crimson blossoms, glowing like rubies amidst the emerald leaves. And on the topmost twig perched a bird of flame, still singing, its scarlet plumage brighter than the sunrise.

And the wind came again and whispered to all the creatures, "See, this is the reward of faith and hope and constancy." To the bush it murmured, "Green is the color of life and red is the color of sacrifice. Wear these hues forever." And to the bird: "Scarlet stands for the trumpet-sound of courage, and for steadfastness. Wear this badge until time is no more."

So it was, and so it still is. We call the bush the camellia now, and the bird the cardinal. But what we call them doesn't matter; they are what they are.

This is the story they tell to this day in the Georgia low-country where I was born. They tell it every year, yes, every year when Christmas draws near. And some of us believe it may be true. ❊

The Donkey

VAN VARNER

He was not a handsome animal, this donkey. His ears were too long, his body too squat, and his flanks were scarred with the welts of many beatings. He was a common creature, his coat the color of dust, dingy, far from the ivory white hues reserved, as Scripture said, for the mounts of royalty. Common he was, yet solid, standing wearily in the cold stable, his muzzle deep in barley, the rich-wet sounds of munching loud in the darkness.

Someone came into the stable. There was a rush of activity. The donkey's ears pricked as he heard the voice of the man, his most recent owner. "Wake up," the man whispered to the lady as a tiny light burst through the darkness. "Bring the Baby. We must go now. Quickly."

The man came to him and adjusted the rope that served as his halter. This was a good man. The best. No beatings from him. No whips. No kicks. No cries of "Stupid beast!" Over and over again during the three tiring days of travel from Galilee, the man had patted him. "Good fellow," he'd said as the donkey picked his way skillfully among the rocks on the rude trail. The man had been gentle, too, with the lady. She had been heavy with child then.

The man led the donkey out into the open air. The sun was just beginning to appear. The lady came out, bearing in her arms a small bundle that she held close and tight. "But where?" she asked the man, fearfully.

"South," said the man. "Egypt, if we can."

The lady drew near the donkey and, as the man prepared to help her mount his back, the donkey saw the Child for the first time, and the Child the donkey. In one quick moment the Child reached out and touched the donkey's short, coarse mane. The donkey shivered.

The lady settled on the donkey's back. "Good fellow," said the man as he gave the donkey a pat. And then they were off, the man, the lady, the Child, the donkey.

The morning sun was brightening the earth now, and as its first rays fell upon the retreating figure of the old donkey, they seemed to shimmer. Something had happened to the animal, an extraordinary change. There was pride in the lift of his head; his hooves rose and fell in clean, sharp beats; and his coat—no longer was it the color of dusk. Now the donkey's entire body was of a hue befitting a royal passenger, the color of ivory. ❇

Right Time, Right Place

A Christmas Kitten

ALICE LEEDY MASON

Our Christmas kitten's really bright;
She's standing guard this Christmas night.
Sometimes she jumps from stair to stair
Or hides beneath the rocking chair.

She's keeping watch from dusk till dawn;
Something moves and the chase is on!
Papers rustle in a box;
A search is made of Christmas socks.

A toy mouse, a catnip ball,
Some scraps of yarn out in the hall,
The Christmas crèche, a cookie plate,
All these she must investigate.

But not just now—it's time for bed;
A place to lay her weary head.
Content this is the place for her,
She drops her guard and starts to purr!

A Puppy Named Maxx

Suzan Davis

*A*s soon as my daughters and I walked into the house, they started in on me again. "So, Mom, can we get a dog?" Katelyn, thirteen, said.

"Yeah, Mom," Savannah, eleven, echoed. "Pleeease?"

They'd been after me for weeks. I'd even overheard them asking for a puppy in their bedtime prayers. The last thing in the world I wanted to do was disappoint my daughters, but I was a busy single mom. I had enough on my plate. "C'mon, you guys," I said, glancing at the answering machine. The message light was blinking. "We already have a dog."

Duke, our beagle-corgi mix, lifted his head from his bed, as if he knew we were talking about him. Good old Duke. At six, he was as sweet as could be, but not exactly a bundle of energy. He hardly ever got up to greet us anymore.

"We need a dog we can play with, Mom," Katelyn said. "A puppy. This family isn't big enough."

I felt a pang of guilt. I'd promised myself the girls wouldn't miss out on anything after their dad and I were separated. My teaching schedule at a local college gave me plenty of time to be with my daughters, and I thought I'd done a pretty good job raising them. Still, doubts had a way of creeping in. Especially now, with the holidays around the corner. Everyone else was planning big family get-togethers. It was just me and my girls. Could I really give them everything they needed?

"Maybe Santa will bring us a puppy next month," said Savannah hopefully.

"A Chihuahua," Katelyn added. "Like in *Legally Blonde*."

"Now that I draw the line at," I said. "There are too many coyotes around here. If we do get a dog, it's got to be bigger than a dinner entrée." I hit the play button on the answering machine.

The message was from our neighbor. "Hi, Suzan. Want a dog?"

The girls whooped and hollered. I was trapped. How could I say no? Our neighbor was always rescuing animals. This time, it turned out to be a four-month-old German shepherd. The girls forgot all about Chihuahuas and immediately dubbed him Wolfgang Günter Klaus von Schneiderheim. Wolfie for short.

Wolfie wasn't with us a week before I was every bit as in love with him as the girls were. Who knew I'd take such pleasure in being followed around by this floppy-eared goofball with his funny, lopsided gait? He'd trail me from room to room, out to the front gate to get the mail, everywhere. Even Duke seemed to approve of the new arrival, thumping his tail whenever Wolfie came over to give him a sniff. Wolfie didn't like being separated from us for a second, so I took him with me to work at the college. Like some of my students, he didn't take notes and had a tendency to fall asleep during my lectures. Yes, it was my daughters who had prayed for a puppy, but Wolfie ended up filling a space in my life too. *Lord, thank You for sending Wolfie to complete our family.*

A few weeks before Christmas, Wolfie's odd gait turned into a pronounced limp. And he was only picking at his food. I took him to the veterinarian.

He gave Wolfie a full exam and took X-rays. "This is bad, Suzan," he said. "I noticed Wolfie's hips were narrow. This X-ray shows why. Wolfie was born without any hip sockets. His back legs are poking into him whenever he walks. He's in constant pain. That's why he's not eating. We'll get a second opinion, but don't expect it to be good news."

It wasn't. The only humane thing to do, the other vets I consulted informed me, was put Wolfie down. As unexpectedly as he had come into our lives, Wolfie would be leaving us.

On December 15, Wolfie passed away peacefully, snuggled in Savannah's and my arms. The girls and I cried a bucket of tears. I did my best to make Christmas a happy one for my daughters, but it was no use. Wolfie's absence cast a pall over everything.

I thought a day out at a shopping center—we'd have a nice lunch and then hit the after-Christmas sales—might cheer them up. But outside one store was a line of SPCA cages full of dogs that needed homes. Savannah picked up a puppy and held it close, as if trying to fill up the hole left by Wolfie's loss.

Katelyn couldn't even look at the dogs. "Mom, can we get out of here?" she pleaded. "They all just remind me of Wolfie."

Lord, I prayed, *I thought Wolfie was supposed to complete our family. Now what am I going to do?*

Halfway home, my cell phone went off. It was a young woman named Dana Swain, the leader of a Girl Scout troop in town.

"Suzan, I found your dog."

Our dog?

"I'm sorry, Dana, what did you say?"

"He was standing in the middle of Auburn-Folsom Road with cars whizzing by on both sides. But don't worry, I got him. I'll drop him off. Inside your fence, so he can't get out again."

Auburn-Folsom Road was a full mile from our house. How had sleepy old Duke mustered the energy to get that far? We pulled up to our house. Sure enough, there was a dog standing behind the fence.

Not Duke. A wet, muddy German shepherd puppy.

"He looks just like Wolfie!" Savannah cried. "Are we in the twilight zone?" We walked through the gate and the puppy jumped on the girls, covering them with licks. I opened our front door. The puppy charged into the house without a moment's pause. He sniffed Duke (who didn't seem to mind) and then sat and looked up at me expectantly. I set out some water and food. He inhaled the kibble so quickly the girls burst into peals of laughter.

I called Dana and told her this couldn't be our dog because we'd had to put Wolfie down. "I'm sorry, I had no idea," she said. "When I saw that shepherd puppy in the middle of the road, I figured it had to be yours."

It was easy to see why. He could have been Wolfie's twin. If we were in the twilight zone, like Savannah said, for the moment I didn't care. After weeks of sadness, our house was full of joy again.

Not for long. Early the next morning, Dana called again. "I hate to tell you, but I saw a sign at the market just now. About a lost four-month-old shepherd." She gave me the owner's number.

I forced myself to dial it. This call was going to break my daughters' hearts.

"Oh, I'm so glad you have my dog," the woman said. "I'll be right over."

I went into the girls' room. They were asleep, with the already christened Noah Maximillion von Swain, or Maxx, curled up at the foot of Katelyn's bed.

I woke the girls and broke the news. "The owner will be here soon," I said.

"Mom," Savannah said, "I've got almost nine hundred dollars saved up in my bank account. Do you think if I give it to the lady she'll let us keep Maxx?"

"Honey, it's not about money. It's about where the dog belongs."

Savannah turned and buried her face in Maxx's neck.

The owner arrived. Katelyn and Savannah watched, not saying a word, as she threw her arms around Maxx.

"Thank you so much," she said. "This dog wasn't at my house an hour before he ran away."

Maxx padded over to my daughters and plopped down between them.

"We had a German shepherd," said Katelyn. "Just like this one. He died right before Christmas."

The woman looked at the dog and my two girls for a long moment.

"I wanted an eight-week-old female," she said. "But somehow yesterday I found myself buying this four-month-old male. I put him in my backyard, and an hour later he'd vanished. My fence has held plenty of dogs over the years. Not one of them ever got out. I couldn't understand it. Well, now I do. This puppy was looking for the right family. And he's found it. You know, I think God chose him for you."

I think so too. We single mothers take all the help we can get. Did I say I was raising my daughters all on my own? Not by a long shot. ❄

The Christmas Day Kitten

JAMES HERRIOT

hristmas can never go by without my remembering a certain little cat. I first saw her when I called to see one of Mrs. Pickering's most loved Basset hounds.

I looked in some surprise at the furry creature moving quietly down the hall.

"I didn't know you had a cat," I said to Mrs. Pickering, who was a plumpish, pleasant-faced woman.

Mrs. Pickering smiled. "We haven't really. Debbie is a stray. She comes here two or three times a week and we give her some food. I don't know where she lives."

"Do you ever get the feeling that she wants to stay with you?" I asked.

"No." Mrs. Pickering shook her head. "She's a timid little thing. Just creeps in, has some food, and then slips away. She doesn't seem to want to let me help her in any way."

I looked at the little tabby cat again. "But she isn't just having food today."

"It's a funny thing, but every now and again she pops through into the sitting-room and sits by the fire for a few minutes. It's as though she was giving herself a treat."

The little cat was sitting very upright on the thick rug that lay in front of the fireplace in which the coals glowed and flamed. The three Bassets were already lying there, but they seemed used to Debbie because two of them sniffed her in a bored manner and the third merely cocked a sleepy eye at her before flopping back to sleep.

Debbie made no effort to curl up or wash herself or do anything other than gaze quietly ahead. This was obviously a special event in her life, a treat.

Then suddenly she turned and crept from the room without a sound and was gone. "That's just the way it is with Debbie," said Mrs. Pickering, laughing. "She never stays more than ten minutes or so, and then she's off."

I often visited the Pickering home and I always looked out for the little cat. On one occasion I spotted her nibbling daintily from a saucer at the kitchen door. As I watched, she turned and almost floated on light footsteps into the hall and then through into the sitting-room.

Debbie settled herself in the middle of the pile of Basset hounds in her usual way: upright, still and gazing into the glowing fire.

This time, I tried to make friends with her, but she leaned away as I stretched out my hand. However, I talked to her softly and managed to stroke her cheek with one finger.

Then it was time for her to go and, once outside the house, she jumped up on to the stone wall and down the other side. The last I saw was the little tabby figure flitting away across the grassy field.

"I wonder where she goes," I murmured.

"That's something we've never been able to find out," said Mrs. Pickering.

It was three months later that I next heard from Mrs. Pickering—and it happened to be Christmas morning.

"I'm so sorry to bother you today of all days," said Mrs. Pickering apologetically.

"Don't worry at all," I said. "Which of the dogs needs attention?"

"It's not the dogs. It's . . . Debbie. She's come to the house, and there's something very wrong. Please come quickly."

I drove through the empty market square. The snow was thick on the road and on the roofs of the surrounding houses. The shops were closed but the pretty colored lights of the Christmas trees winked in the windows.

Mrs. Pickering's house was beautifully decorated with tinsel and holly, and the rich smell of turkey and sage and onion stuffing wafted from the kitchen. But she had a very worried look on her face as she led me through to the sitting-room.

Debbie was there but she wasn't sitting upright in her usual position. She was lying quite still—and huddled close to her lay a tiny kitten.

I looked in amazement. "What have we got here?"

"It's the strangest thing," Mrs. Pickering replied. "I haven't seen her for several weeks and then she came in about two hours ago, staggered into the kitchen, and she was carrying the kitten in her mouth. She brought it in here and laid it on the rug. Almost immediately I could see she wasn't well. Then she lay down like this and she hasn't moved since."

I knelt on the rug and passed my hand over Debbie's body, which Mrs. Pickering had placed on a piece of sheet. She was very, very thin, and her coat was dirty. I knew she didn't have long to live.

"Is she ill, Mr. Herriot?" asked Mrs. Pickering in a trembling voice.

"Yes . . . yes, I'm afraid so. But I don't think she is in any pain."

Mrs. Pickering looked at me, and I saw there were tears in her eyes. Then she knelt beside Debbie and stroked the cat's head while the tears fell on her dirty fur.

"Oh, the poor little thing! I should have done more for her."

I spoke gently, "Nobody could have done more than you. Nobody could have been kinder. And see, she has brought her kitten to you, hasn't she?"

"Yes, you are right, she has." Mrs. Pickering reached out and lifted up the tiny, bedraggled kitten. "Isn't it strange—Debbie knew she was dying so she brought her kitten here. And on Christmas Day."

I bent down and put my hand on Debbie's heart. There was no beat. "I'm afraid she has died." I lifted the feather-light body, wrapped it in the piece of sheet and took it out to the car.

When I came back, Mrs. Pickering was still stroking the kitten. The tears had dried, and she was bright-eyed as she looked at me.

"I've never had a cat before," she said.

I smiled, "Well, it looks as though you've got one now."

And she certainly had. The kitten grew rapidly into a sleek handsome and bouncy tabby cat and Mrs. Pickering called him Buster. He wasn't timid like his little mother and he lived like a king—and with the ornate collar he always wore, looked like one too.

I watched him grow up with delight, but the occasion that always stays in my mind was the following Christmas Day, a year after his arrival.

I was on my way home after visiting a farmer with a sick cow and I was looking forward to my Christmas dinner. Mrs. Pickering was at her front door when I passed her house, and I heard her call out, "Merry Christmas, Mr. Herriot! Come in and have a drink to warm you up."

I had a little time to spare, but I stopped the car and went in. In the house there was all the festive cheer of last year and the same glorious whiff of sage and onion stuffing. But this year, there was no sorrow—there was Buster!

He was darting up to each of the Basset hounds in turn, ears pricked, eyes twinkling, dabbing a paw at them and then streaking away.

Mrs. Pickering laughed. "Buster does tease them so. He gives them no peace."

She was right. For a long time, the dogs had led a rather sedate life: gentle walks with their mistress, plenty of good food, and long snoring sessions on the rugs and armchairs. Then Buster arrived.

He was now dancing up to the youngest dog again, head on one side, asking him to play. When he started boxing with both paws, it was too much for the Basset, who rolled over with the cat in a wrestling game.

"Come into the garden," said Mrs. Pickering. "I want to show you something."

She lifted a hard rubber ball from the sideboard, and we went outside.

She threw the ball across the lawn, and Buster bounded after it over the frosty grass, his tabby coat gleaming in the sun. He seized the ball in his mouth, brought it back to his mistress, dropped it at her feet and waited. Mrs. Pickering threw it and again Buster brought it back.

I gasped. A retriever cat!

The Bassets looked on unimpressed. Nothing would ever make *them* chase a ball, but Buster did it again and again as though he would never tire of it.

Mrs. Pickering turned to me. "Have you ever seen anything like that?"

"No," I replied. "He is a most remarkable cat."

We went back into the house, where she held Buster close to her, laughing as the big cat purred loudly. Looking at him, so healthy and contented, I remembered his mother who had carried her tiny kitten to the only place of comfort and warmth she had ever known.

Mrs. Pickering was thinking the same thing because she turned to me and, although she was smiling, her eyes were thoughtful. "Debbie would be pleased," she said.

I nodded. "Yes, she would. It was just a year ago today she brought him in, wasn't it?"

"That's right." She hugged Buster again. "The best Christmas present I've ever had." ❄

Igabella, the Perfect Present

*T*he Valley Mall was bustling with holiday shoppers preparing to celebrate Christmas. Seated at a table in front of the bookstore, I was enjoying the flurry of activity at a book signing for my first published children's book. I never suspected I would soon be making a decision to add another member to our family's menagerie!

But then Denise and her twin sister Dawn appeared, accompanied by their mother. The two young teens giggled and fidgeted in front of the table. Their dark brown eyes sparkled.

"Mom thought I should ask your permission," Denise began. "Would you mind if I gave Mike an iguana for Christmas?"

Before I could reply, she added, "Mike says he has always wanted an iguana. It would be the perfect present!"

"I don't know a thing about iguanas," I protested, not wanting to dampen her enthusiasm, but feeling more vulnerable than skeptical.

"They just eat romaine lettuce. They're really no trouble at all," Denise quickly reassured me. "It will have a heat rock in a little terrarium. Mike could keep it on his desk."

Helplessly, I looked at Mrs. Webb.

"I thought she should check first with you," Mrs. Webb said, with wisdom that should have made it easier for me to graciously suggest another gift option.

Denise excitedly added, "The pet store here even has iguanas for sale today. Oh, please, Mrs. Baumgardner!" she pleaded. "It would be the perfect gift."

She knew I would agree. I couldn't deny my son "the perfect gift," could I? Of course, I was sworn to secrecy.

Mike named the iguana "Iggy" until months later when she surprised us by laying twenty-eight eggs. From then on, she was dubbed "Igabella."

And Igabella was, indeed, the perfect gift! Mike was totally surprised to receive her. He was thrilled with her. She walked out of her cage, up his arm, and traveled around atop his head. Mike fed her, kept her cage clean, purchased special food and supplements for her. He trimmed her nails and even let her splash in the shower! He made friends with the manager of the produce section of the grocery store so there was always an abundance of outer leaves of romaine lettuce for Igabella.

Our entire family was fascinated by this scaly green creature. Her spine was covered with spikes and she had a hood. There were turquoise-colored disks on either side of her head. Her eyes had a wise, yet quizzical look. I spoke to her, believing she could understand me. The expression in her eyes convinced me she did.

I took many photographs of Igabella: Igabella on the kitchen table, Igabella peeking from behind a potted plant, Igabella perched atop Mike's head. Perhaps it was because I sketched her that it seemed we communicated.

As Mike outgrew his clothes and shoes, so Igabella outgrew several cages! By the time Mike graduated from high school and left home for art school, Igabella was ensconced in a large, part-wooden, part-Plexiglas cabinet in the family room. Pets were not allowed in Mike's apartment, so I became Igabella's "guardian."

On Mike's visits home from school, he would rush to check on Igabella. She had grown quite large, perhaps four feet in length, including her tail.

As much as I enjoyed Igabella, I always felt guilty about her being confined to a cage. Sometimes we would let her go out into the room. She would climb to the top of the curtain rods or perch on the shelf of a bookcase. She never seemed to want to explore very far away from her cage. Perhaps she considered it "home" and was comfortable and contented.

Tragedy struck our family on June 8, 1998. At just twenty years of age, our precious Michael was killed in an automobile accident. "Take good care of Igabella for me," he had instructed me before he returned to school that last weekend. And so I did.

A year later, our older son, Matthew, and his fiancée Gretchen were to be married at our home. Mike's twin brother Mark was to be best man. Among the many preparations made for the wedding was that of painting the family room. We moved Igabella's "apartment" outside so the paint fumes wouldn't harm her.

It was when I went to feed her that I discovered she was gone. Somehow she must have been able to push against the Plexiglas door and escape. We searched. I called her name. She was "on the lam," no doubt. She had tasted freedom and was nowhere to be found.

Iguanas are arboreal, which means they love climbing trees. Huge trees surround our home, which adjoins acres of woods. It was summer and the weather was perfect for Igabella, if she had to escape. I just hoped she would return before cold weather.

I didn't know much about the mentality of an iguana, but somehow I knew Igabella would come back. We left her apartment outside, with the door open. I would call for her, hoping she might respond to my voice. But the summer passed, and Igabella remained at large. Nights began to get very cold. We had a frost.

It was a chilly morning in late October when my husband was giving the lawn a final mowing. Suddenly, he burst into the kitchen, holding something in his arms—Igabella. She was barely alive. He had found her in the grass at the base of a tree.

I rushed upstairs and put several large towels in the dryer. I wrapped her in the warm towels and cradled her in my arms like a baby. I talked to her, encouraging her to make an effort to recover.

Oh yes, I told Igabella how much I loved her and that she was very special to me. It seemed incredible that she had returned. I thought of how wonderful it was that she had had her freedom all summer. Surely, she must have watched us from those treetops. I thought she probably even saw the wedding!

Igabella gave me her wise, yet quizzical look. Somehow, as I talked to her and held her in those warm towels, I felt as if Mike were watching us. And when she became stiff in my arms and her eyes closed, it seemed as if, once again, she was perched atop Mike's head. I could even see him grinning as he showed off his Igabella to the heavenly host. ❄

Bill's Christmas Miracle

*I*n the basement of my apartment building in New York City, I discovered a colony of wild cats. Moved by their plight, I began feeding them, but conditions down there became so that the cats were all infested with fleas and getting sick. One by one I trapped them, took them to the vet, and had them cleaned up, inoculated and neutered.

One of them, a female I named Cleopatra, I brought home to my family, but she was so feral that I had to keep her locked up in the bathroom so she wouldn't attack my other cats. I tried to get close to her, to stroke her and to show her that she wasn't in any danger, that she had found a home and that she was loved. But she didn't trust anybody. Cleo wouldn't let me even touch her; she clawed me and bit me whenever I got too close. My hands and arms were covered in scratches and teeth marks.

Finally, when she had calmed down somewhat, I thought it was time to let Cleo have access to the rest of the apartment. The moment she was out of the bathroom, she dashed under my bed and wouldn't leave, hiding there, refusing to come out even to eat. I wound up putting a food bowl and a litter pan under the bed, but that was an unsatisfactory arrangement.

What I really wanted was to have Cleo join the family and be my pet, but I saw that I'd have to start from scratch (and I mean scratch!). Figuring she'd have to go back to confinement in the bathroom for a while, I set up a small cat carrier there and pushed her food dish farther and farther back into it with each meal.

On Christmas Eve 1995, I decided to attend the Blessing of the Animals at Central Presbyterian Church—and to bring her along with me. Maybe in the presence of all those contented animals and devoted animal lovers Cleo would feel safe and begin to calm down and not be so frightened. I have always believed there is something divine in the communion between people and animals—maybe this would bring it out in Cleo.

That evening, before going to the blessing, I sat and meditated, focusing entirely on the hope that Cleopatra would heal and be unafraid, that she would someday allow me to touch her.

With Cleo in the carrier, I took the subway from Brooklyn to Manhattan to the Central Presbyterian Church on Park Avenue and Sixty-Fourth Street. On the train I took off my glove, baring my hand laced with scars and scratches, and tentatively opened Cleo's box. Slowly, I put my bare hand in and touched her very lightly on the back, and—

Nothing. No hissing, no biting, none of her usual wild and frantic scratching. No distrust at all. Just an amazing peace and quiet and the feel of her warm fur under my fingers.

My heart leaped as I realized that for the first time Cleopatra was allowing me to pet her. All during the train ride, I stroked her quietly. Once we were in the church, the woman sitting next to me put her hand into the carrier and stroked Cleo. Cleo accepted the stroking quietly and without resistance. On the train ride home from the blessing, it occurred to me that I had a new cat. A shy, scared cat, but my cat.

That night, I was asleep in bed when I woke up to a weight pressing against me. It was Cleo, curled up against my body and purring like a small engine as Christmas morning came. A great feeling of relief and gratitude washed over me as I received this little creature's love. From that night on, it was as though she'd always been with me and had never once been wild. All her fears were forgotten. Cleo was a sweet, gentle, loving pussycat. She was home.

To this day, I believe Cleo was a gift from God. My Christmas miracle. ❈

Barney McCabe

SHARON AZAR

arney McCabe, I called him. I found him tied to a storefront on Christmas Day, starving and shivering, abandoned to the streets. I'd seen so many like him before. I had been rescuing dogs for a long time, starting with Baby Bear.

Walking through a city park one afternoon, I saw a large Belgian sheepdog tied to a tree. His tongue drooped from his mouth like a tag on a marked-down dress. A cardboard sign read: "Owner died. Please take dog. Very friendly." His long, shaggy locks were well groomed and he was obviously well fed. Would I take him? Something made me say yes.

I didn't know much about dogs except they needed to be walked and fed. Taking Baby Bear out in my concrete-and-asphalt neighborhood, I met other dog owners who stopped and gave me advice. Children couldn't help hugging Baby Bear. I made a whole new set of friends.

"Sharon," one of them said to me one day, "I found an abandoned dog down by the river. Can you help me look for a new home for him?"

"Sure," I said. "Whatever I can do." With that I became part of a network of dog rescuers. We posted signs on trees, traded phone calls and passed information from one to another. It felt like a calling, something God wanted me to do—to give these lonely, often abused animals a new lease on life. Soon I was taking care of dogs for a night or two, until they could be placed, or going on trips to the vet with a foster pet in tow, making sure it was healthy enough for a new home. Some of the dogs stayed.

First came Fonzie, a large male husky someone had left in front of the Metropolitan Museum of Art. One of the curators urged him on me, with a few dollars for his care.

Next came Ginger. I had just lost Baby Bear to old age. Both Fonzie and I were grief-stricken, so when we met a man in the park giving up an eight-month-old border collie/golden retriever mix, I decided to take her home.

Then came Barney. My friend Norman and I were on our way to a party that Christmas Day several years ago. Bundled up against a bitter wind coming off the Hudson, we made our way through the slushy streets. As we passed the local pet store, I saw a black dog roped to the door. The store was closed.

I knelt down with my hands open. The poor creature was trembling uncontrollably, head down against the knifelike wind. His ribs protruded through his dull coat and there were scars on his body. He looked to be part German shepherd and part Labrador.

"It's okay, boy," I said softly. He looked at me, his eyes wary.

"Sharon?" Norman said. I knew what he was concerned about: *You don't have room for another dog, especially a big one like this.* He was right, but it was Christmas Day, and I couldn't just walk away.

I let the dog sniff my hand, still talking softly. You could tell he was torn between his fear of people and his instinct for shelter. I cautiously untied the leash, careful not to startle him. "It'll only be for a few days," I told Norman. "Until I can find a home for him." At my apartment I put the stray in the bedroom, away from the other two dogs, left him some food and water and closed the door.

I had no idea what my bedroom would look like when I got home from the party. There was no telling what a scared, abused animal would do, locked in. After greeting Fonzie and Ginger, I edged into the bedroom. The stray was lying on my bed, paws crossed, his eyes searching my face. Nothing was out of place. Even the bowls were right where I had left them, licked clean.

He proved a good houseguest, but a difficult dog to walk. I had to hold him on a short leash. If anyone raised a hand to wave or made a sudden movement, he growled and snarled. He absolutely refused to be touched by anyone but me.

"Please don't pet the dog," I had to say to children. "Not yet. He's not used to people."

I named him Barney McCabe after a farmer's dog I once knew. But that animal had been playful and good-natured. This one was anxious, distrustful. Living in my small apartment became difficult with three dogs—two of them males who fought for their territory. I continued to keep Barney separate from Ginger and Fonzie.

Until then, rescuing dogs had brought me so much comfort and satisfaction. But I wondered if I was in over my head. Even if I wanted to, I couldn't put Barney up for adoption. He was so damaged, so afraid of people. *Lord,* I prayed, *tell me what you want me to do with this dog.*

"Barney," I told my charge, "you just need to be loved." I had always believed that love healed all wounds, yet Barney's seemed so deep.

Then came Dane. Not a stray dog, but a little boy. He was a sweet-faced eight-year-old who lived with his family in a nearby apartment. He loved the country, and he longed for the freedom of opening a door and running out into a backyard. He'd also recently lost a cat and he missed it terribly.

"Hi, Sharon!" he'd call whenever he saw me on the street with my dogs. He rushed over when he spotted me walking my new dog.

"Don't pet him," I warned.

"What's his name?" Dane asked.

"Barney McCabe," I said. Dane stood still and let Barney sniff. Barney's tail wagged almost imperceptibly.

Dane began a ritual. When I came home after work, Dane was waiting outside. First we took Ginger and Fonzie for a walk, and then we walked Barney. Before long I was letting Dane hold his leash. Back inside the apartment, Dane played with the dogs. He wrestled with Fonzie or played tug-of-war with Ginger. All the while, Barney looked on.

One spring day Dane showed up with a pocket full of dog biscuits. He gave some to the other two dogs; then he looked at me and asked, "May I?"

"Go ahead."

"Barney, sit," he said. Barney obeyed. "Okay, now, here's a dog biscuit. It's for you. Take it." He held the treat out. Barney leaned forward and gobbled it right from his open palm.

Watching the two of them, I couldn't help wondering, *God, is that what you'd planned all along?* Barney was to be Dane's friend. I couldn't have guessed that on Christmas Day, and I certainly couldn't have known the role I would play.

"Good dog," Dane said. And then Barney nuzzled the boy's neck and licked his ear. ❄

The Gift of Lucy

LONNIE HULL DUPONT

*S*he came to me on a cold windy night the week before Thanksgiving, and I heard her before I saw her. The wind chill was thirteen degrees, unseasonably cold even for Michigan, and yet somebody abandoned her—a five-month-old kitten—near my house.

I had just finished running errands that frigid evening and had holidays on my mind as I wove through the remote roads home. My husband Joe and I had moved from California to an old brick tank of a house in southern Michigan only a few years before.

It was dark as I pulled into the driveway. The shadowy tops of the maple trees standing guard around the house shook audibly in the wind. I looked forward to getting inside to curl up with our cat Kit Kat, a beautiful and husky tortoiseshell who had come to us one night in the rain the previous year. Together we would watch for Joe to come home from work.

As I turned off the engine, my thoughts turned to the happy fact that next week would be the one to pull out the Christmas decorations. When Joe and I had married six years earlier, we vowed, among other things, to redeem Christmas for one another, because years of moving around geographically as single individuals had made that holiday difficult for each of us.

Before we met, I handled being far away from family during major holidays by inviting every other stray reveler I knew to my one-bedroom apartment in San Francisco. I had lived in Europe one year, and the expatriates there had taught me that the way to handle holidays away from home was to over-celebrate. It was a good suggestion. When I moved back to the States and eventually to California alone, I made it a tradition to over-celebrate holidays.

In San Francisco, it wasn't unusual to have fifteen people in my one-bedroom apartment for a sit-down Thanksgiving dinner—friends and strangers both. At Christmas, there were many get-togethers during the season, and I watched to see who might need company on Christmas day. I would invite a few of them over, and we would cook, talk, keep the fireplace stoked and watch the fog drift over the hills. While I built my own traditions, I built them alone. And it was fine.

Joe and I had a whirlwind courtship. We met in August, began dating in September and fell in love by Thanksgiving. He proposed to me three days before Christmas, and on Christmas Day we called our relatives and friends to tell them we were getting married. On that day, we promised one another we would always make Christmas our best time. No more celebrating far from family. Now *we* were family.

For me, the holiday thrill started with hauling out the boxes of Christmas things the day after Thanksgiving. Among them, my childhood doll dressed in Christmas finery. A macramé wreath made by a former student. A huge papier-mâché crèche with a Madonna that looked so much like Mary Queen of Scots that an artist friend in San Francisco offered to paint her to look more authentic. Vintage ceramic block letters that spelled NOEL, except after New Year's parties when I always found them spelling LEON.

And tree ornaments. I had collected them for years without ever getting a Christmas tree. My single days were good ones, but there were some things I'd never liked doing alone, and one of them was putting up a Christmas tree. So I hung ornaments on the fireplace. If ever I had an old-fashioned hope chest, it was my box of tree ornaments.

Now, in Michigan, Joe and I would drive our old station wagon to a nearby farm and pick out a tree. At home, he put the tree up in our dining room with its thirteen-feet-high ceiling while I unpacked the ornaments I'd collected over the years.

Joe and I formed another new tradition together in Michigan. We took the week off between Christmas and New Years and made virtually no plans. During that week, we hid out and took a home vacation. We looked forward to it every year.

So my thoughts were all about holidays this cold November evening when I stepped out of my car. Then I heard it. The wind came heartily from the southwest and blustered around the corner of the house, and with it came a sound I didn't want to hear—the cry of a small animal.

A stray cat? I hoped not. When we first moved into the house, I'd prepared myself for dropped-off cats. I remembered them well from a childhood in the country. But during my years away from Michigan, the Department of Natural Resources had introduced coyotes to the area, and farmers now claimed these critters picked off the barn cats and the strays.

Besides the coyotes, there were other dangers at our home. Our house sat on a winding two-lane highway with plenty of semitruck traffic, speedy and fierce. Kit Kat had been the only stray from our place who managed to survive long enough for us to adopt her. And then there was the weather.

I braced against the wind and rounded the house. As soon as the back door light flashed on, out of the blackness sprang the most gorgeous kitten I had ever seen. She was a solid smoky blue-gray and so beautiful and so panicked that I'm embarrassed to say I actually burst into tears.

The kitten beat me to the door and expressed tremendous relief at seeing me by rubbing back and forth on my ankles and loudly purring. She apparently had been around people enough to know to come to them for protection, and she was using everything in her power to get it. I put down my bags and bent down to pet her. Then I gently pushed her away from me while I unlocked the door to the house, and I had quite a time keeping her from going in. I told her I'd be right back, and I nudged her away with the toe of my shoe. Indoors, I opened a can of cat food and filled a dish of water.

When I opened the door again, I saw that the kitten had managed to tuck herself in between the storm door and the back door, and there she huddled on the threshold, trying to get warm. This broke my heart. I nudged her gently off the threshold and stepped back outside with her, talking in soothing tones. I placed the dishes on the deck, and she hunkered down to eat. Then I sneaked back indoors and watched her from the window.

The problem was that Joe and I already had Kit Kat, and we really didn't believe we could have another pet. Kit Kat was a tough little thing. I met a guy once who laughingly described his cat as one who carried a knife, and in some respects, we probably could have said the same about Kit Kat, even though all that toughness housed a truly soulful creature.

But Kit Kat had fended for herself outside too long to get along with competition. She was an absolute sweetheart unless confronted by another creature, and then that swamp cat was in full form. She backed my mother's dog right into a corner. So we never considered bringing in another cat—we figured on her own territory, Kit Kat would kill the competition. We did not yet know that housecats don't kill each other; we were pretty green to the world of felines.

I saw Joe pull up as the kitten continued to work her way through the dish of food. Joe walked in the door and looked at me. "So what's the story out there?"

I didn't know what was wrong with me, but I started crying again. "She's a stray," I blubbered. "We can't leave her out there or she'll freeze to death. And we can't have her inside with Kit Kat. She'll kill her."

Joe thought for a minute. "Let's put her upstairs in that room we just painted." Our upstairs was separated from the downstairs by a door, and we didn't yet use the upstairs rooms. We had indeed just cleaned out and painted one bedroom there. "We have another litter box," Joe continued. "Let's put the kitten in the empty room until we can figure out what to do with her. At least she'll be warm and safe, and Kit Kat won't be able to get to her."

It was a fine plan. "Okay," I sniffed. I put Kit Kat in the basement as Joe headed out the back door. When he brought in the kitten, her purr was so noisy it preceded her like an announcement.

"Careful," Joe said, "her nose is bleeding." We wrapped her in my pink bath towel, and I held her on her back like a baby. Oh happiness! The kitten purred and wiggled, and tears sprang up in me again. I felt like an idiot.

"I don't know if she's bleeding from her nose or if it's a scrape," Joe observed, looking her over. We noted she was a female, around five months old, short-haired with a soft, thick coat. She was the shade of gray that cat people call blue, from her triangular head to her tapered paws, even her straight nose and velvety ears. She gazed back and forth at us, sea-green eyes peering out of that smoky coat like headlights in fog.

"Wow," said Joe. "This cat could be in a calendar." Indeed, she was perfectly and beautifully made. We *ooh*ed and *ah*ed over her, and I started to calm down once I realized her sweet nature and exceptional beauty would guarantee her a home with someone. It was hard to imagine anyone abandoning this lovely creature with what seemed to be a winning personality.

Eventually Joe took her from me. "I'll get her bedded down," he offered. "She's probably exhausted."

Never was there a happier feline than the blue kitten that night. We made her a bed in a box with an old sweater of mine to keep her warm, and Joe took her upstairs. Joe fixed up a litter box for her, and she leaped right in and had a private moment. She devoured another bowl of food, purring the entire time, and then curled up in her new bed and watched Joe putter around her new room from under heavy eyelids. Her relief at being able to safely relax was palpable.

I stayed downstairs on the phone trying to find her a home. For hours I called everyone I knew, to no avail. So I told Joe he would have to be the one to tend to the kitten so I could avoid getting attached to her. He agreed to it.

The next morning, when Joe went upstairs to feed the kitten, he saw that she had cleaned herself up. Now it was clear that her nose was merely scraped. In a few days, we took her to our vet for a check-up and vaccinations. She purred through the entire appointment—even during the shots.

The kitten stayed upstairs in her room for the next several days while we tried to find her a home. One evening after a week had passed, Joe put Kit Kat in the basement and then brought the kitten downstairs, thinking I might want to hold her. He was right. I had been avoiding her so I would not get attached, but I was itching to touch that soft little creature. I placed her on her back and cradled her in my arms. She let me cuddle her, rub her downy belly, even gently separate and rub each of her toes. She always kept her claws in. At one point she stretched out a front paw and placed it on my cheek, keeping it there while she gazed into my face.

Oh dear. How was I going to give her away?

For the next few weeks, The Little One, as we began calling her, lived in her room. When Joe poured new litter into her box, she climbed onto his shoulder to watch. When he poured dry food into her dish, she dove under the bag and let the food pellets rain on her. When he rolled the trash can to the roadside in the moonlight or raked leaves in the front yard in daylight, she watched from a tall upstairs window. She pounced on any toy we gave her, especially rubber balls—she played and played with them in her otherwise empty room. As for me, I would lie in bed in the room below and listen to the small cat rolling the ball back and forth on the pine floor planks early in the morning and late at night and then scampering after it. My brain connected the ball she was rolling to the name Lucille Ball, and then in my heart, I named the kitten Lucy. But I could not really name a cat I was giving away, so I kept her name to myself.

Meantime, downstairs we began decorating the house for Christmas. We picked out a tall, pungent fraser fir that would allow just enough room for an angel to perch atop it without brushing the ceiling. We let it stand undecorated for a few days so Kit Kat could sniff at it and adjust to it. That had worked well the year before during her first Christmas.

Then I pulled out the ornaments and hung them on the tree. I was careful not to put too many dangling things near the bottom—why tempt fate when there's a cat in the house? Kit Kat settled down on the back of the couch to watch. She tucked in her front paws, inhaled the spicy scent of the tree, and watched the blinking Christmas lights. My indulgent family had sent wrapped gifts for Kit Kat, which we placed under the tree. Of course they would receive back from Kit Kat—what else?—Kit Kat candy bars.

But at the back of my mind nagged the future prospects of The Little One upstairs. Over time, three different families each gave a definite yes. Then at the last minute, for a variety of reasons, none could take her. But I knew that if anyone would hold her just once, they'd walk away with her. I'd fallen in love with her myself.

I gave in and began going upstairs every day, several times per day. The kitten was getting lonely and bored up there by herself, so every day I would play with her and then place her on her back and hold her in my arms like a baby. I'd learned from holding Kit Kat that cats like to be rocked. So I'd rock The Little One, rubbing her chest and belly. She would literally gaze up at me and heave a sigh, the picture of contentment. She'd reach her paw up to my face, sometimes both paws, to press against my chin, purring and looking into my face.

To say I was smitten would be an understatement. But I refused to speak her name out loud. I redoubled my efforts to find her a good home before it became too hard to let her go.

I am a praying person. I pray about many things, but with so much misery in the world, should I beseech God on behalf of one blue kitten in winter? I decided, yes, the creatures of the world are here for reasons beyond my understanding. So as I rocked the kitten, I did pray for her future. And one day after she'd been with us just over a month, I distinctly heard inside, *She's yours.*

I protested inside. "I can't have her. We have Kit Kat."

Again I heard, *She's yours.*

I quieted down and let the idea settle in. I rocked her a bit more and then put her in her box-bed and went downstairs. I called Joe, as I often did in the middle of the day, and without my bringing any of this up, he said to me, "You know, some people here at the office are sure we can get the cats together if we take our time with them. So I was thinking, let's try to keep The Little One. Since we'll be home the week between Christmas and New Year, let's use that time to get her together with Kit Kat."

I was stunned that Joe and I would be so in sync about this. It made perfect sense, and Christmas was only a few days away. Maybe it could work. Maybe The Little One really was ours.

I went back upstairs, picked the kitten up, and for the first time whispered into her satiny ear, "Lucy . . . " She purred and purred, as if she'd always known that was her name.

Starting on Christmas day, based on the advice of a local cat expert, Joe and I put the two cats together for brief periods of time. Several times a day that holiday week, one of us tromped upstairs to get Lucy. Then she made her little bunny hops down the steep steps, her journey slowed because she couldn't stop looking around along the way. We introduced her to Kit Kat; then we put them together a few minutes at a time. Then we tried for a half hour, then an hour, and then a few hours.

During these downstairs sessions, we learned that Kit Kat's ferocity actually was an expression of fear of this little ball of fur. But Lucy was fearless about Kit Kat. Sometimes she

ignored Kit Kat in favor of things like flashing lights on the
Christmas tree and ornaments she could bat around the
hardwood floors like a soccer player, but more often she
happily followed Kit Kat around the big house. This decidedly
unnerved Kit Kat. When Kit Kat's adrenaline seemed to rise,
we took Lucy back upstairs.

Slowly but surely, they were tolerating each other. Our pet
expert told us, "When your cats sleep together in the same
room, they're showing they trust each other. If they sleep *on*
each other, your problems are pretty much over." I filed that
away.

The holiday week stretched happily on, and Joe and I
attended a New Year's Eve party. We spied some out-of-town
friends we didn't see very often: Paul and Katie, animal lovers
and foster care providers for their local Humane Society. They
were very interested in the story of Lucy, and they brimmed
with encouragement and approval over what we were doing to
get the two cats used to one another. They assured us we only
needed to give it time.

"Remember how our cat Dandelion acted when we first got
the dog?" Katie said to Paul. She turned to us. "Dandelion
would vomit on the dining room table every time she saw
him." Paul nodded, and they both laughed. Joe and I glanced at

each other in horror. We had a fresh appreciation for our well-behaved Kit Kat.

On the way home, we decided it was time for the two cats to spend some time together without us. By now it seemed apparent that Kit Kat would not harm Lucy, though I still was afraid the curious and rambunctious Lucy would get into some danger by herself. But we had kitten-proofed the place as much as we could. She was six months old now and was going to have to live with us without constant supervision.

So the next day, Joe and I left Lucy downstairs with Kit Kat and went to a New Year's Day family function. We came home after four hours and unlocked the back door. Where was Kit Kat, our greeter?

Joe walked in ahead of me and stopped at the back of an easy chair. As I wriggled out of my coat, he beckoned quietly. I joined him and looked over the top of the chair. There on the seat was our Kit Kat. She was spooned around Lucy, who was curled into a furry ball with her eyes squeezed shut. And Kit Kat was grooming her. Tenderly.

Joe and I grabbed hands and grinned stupidly at one another. Kit Kat stopped her task and looked up at us with the most gentle expression on her face. She held our eyes a moment. Then she turned back to the work of grooming Lucy.

A few weeks before, Lucy had badly needed a home. At the same time, I needed something to cuddle and fuss over, something that needed me back. Joe needed a little playmate to distract him from stress. And Kit Kat needed her own kind to mother and groom and boss around. But for me, Lucy was much more than something to meet our needs. She was a bit of Christmas joy.

Once you become a grown-up, who remembers the Christmas gifts you receive? At the cusp of one Christmas season, Lucy appeared out of the dark and presented herself to me like a personal gift. Of all the many wonderful presents I most likely received that year, the only one I remember is Lucy. ❄

Calling Doctor Trilby

JOHN SHERRILL

*T*here was one thing dog trainer Jeanne Gurnis wished she could have done for her mother before she died. "Mother was in the intensive care unit, and she kept asking to see Corky, her dog," Jeanne recalled. "But the hospital wouldn't hear of it. All I could bring her were photos. She had me prop the pictures on her nightstand so Corky would be the first one to greet her when she woke up, just like at home." Still, Jeanne couldn't help wondering how much more her mother's last days could have been brightened if she'd been able to hug her beloved Corky.

So when a local hospital, Westchester Medical Center, just north of New York City, approached her about starting a pet-therapy program—where specially trained animals would visit patients—Jeanne knew she had to give it a try. "This is only a test," the staff warned her. "We'll have to see if pet therapy really does the patients any good."

The spring of 1999, Jeanne and Trilby, a bright-eyed little corgi who'd been certified through Therapy Dogs

International, became the first volunteer pet-therapy team at the hospital. The staff's initial concerns about infection diminished when they learned Trilby had regular checkups and was bathed and groomed before each visit. And resistance melted away entirely as patients' morale and recovery rate improved measurably after Trilby stopped in to see them.

That December a doctor called Trilby to the intensive care unit to see a patient who seemed beyond medical help. Brain-injured in a car accident, Babs Barter had been in a coma for three weeks. Her husband said she loved dogs, so her doctor decided to try Trilby.

Jeanne knew it was a long shot; patients needed to interact with an animal to benefit. As she and Trilby headed into the ICU, Jeanne prayed, as she often did before a tough assignment, *Father, please guide this visit. Thy will be done.*

Babs was on a ventilator, her motionless body bristling with wires and tubes. With the doctor, head nurse and Babs's husband looking on, Jeanne and Trilby went up to her. "Hello, I'm Jeanne Gurnis. I've brought someone to see you."

Jeanne lifted Trilby onto the bed. "I heard you're a dog lover," Jeanne said. No response. She put Babs's limp hand on the dog's back. "Trilby is a Pembroke Welsh corgi. Want to pet her?"

Still no response. Jeanne kept talking. Twenty minutes passed with no hint of awareness from Babs. "You know, if you don't hold Trilby she might fall off the bed." No reaction. *Lord, what should I do now?* Jeanne wondered.

That's when Trilby took charge. Ever so slowly, the little corgi inched closer to Babs's still body. It was a stretch to suppose that a dog—even one as smart as Trilby—understood what Jeanne was getting at. But then Babs's husband exclaimed, "Look . . . look!"

Jeanne saw it too. Almost imperceptibly, the fingers of the comatose woman moved. "Trilby likes that," Jeanne said to Babs. "Why don't you keep petting her?"

Babs's doctor was so delighted he asked Jeanne and Trilby to come by every day. They did, though Babs's response remained too slight to be sure of.

One morning three weeks after their first visit, Jeanne clearly saw Babs move her fingers. It was unmistakable—she was stroking the dog's soft, thick fur! Two weeks later, Jeanne and Trilby watched Babs's eyes flicker open. When Babs was strong enough to transfer to a rehabilitation center, she got permission for Trilby to visit. Soon Babs was doing so well she was able to go home.

Just before Christmas 2000, a box arrived at Jeanne's house, addressed in a firm, clear hand. "To Trilby Gurnis."

Inside was a huge batch of fresh dog biscuits, and a note from Babs Barter. "Baked by me for Trilby, who saved my life. Thanks for the first-class care." ❄

Just the Right Gift

BARBARA MILLER STREET

I woke up on a December morning with shingles. The pain got worse by the day. I'd done the decorating, but everything else came to a halt. No cooking or baking or celebrating. As far as I was concerned, until I felt better, Christmas was canceled.

Staring out the window, I saw a big, gray cat in the yard, a fuzzy kitten curled by her side. The peaceful scene made me forget myself for a moment. I actually smiled. From then on, I put food out and kept track of our visitors. I felt responsible for them.

Christmas morning dawned bright and beautiful. The mama cat and her baby were asleep beneath the decorated trees on our porch. Christmas spirit welled up in me, and I was reminded of the Mother and Child whose day it really was. A stray gray cat and her fuzzy kitten turned out to be just the gift I needed. ❄

Comfort & Joy

A Christmas Pup

ALICE LEEDY MASON

Oh, what an absolute delight!
Just see what happened Christmas night.
A tiny pup—cute, wiggly, smart—
Came right into my eager heart.

I said "hello" and picked him up;
He was such a naughty pup.
He yawned and tried to get away
Because he thought he'd rather play.

So much to see, so many lights,
A dozen other tempting sights;
He had to wrestle with the rug
Before he paused to give a hug.

He gave each ornament a sniff,
Then tore the bows from every gift.
Worn out at last, he came my way
And love came in my heart to stay.

The Christmas Visit

Jo Coudert

a high point of the second year of the Good
Shepherd Association was a Christmas visit
to a children's hospital that was requested by the
hospital as a special treat for the patients. Paulette and Lana
gathered together ten of their best handlers for an orientation
session in which they described what the handlers were likely
to see and how they might best interact with the
children. "Avoid focusing on the children's appearance," the
handlers were told. "Maintain a positive attitude and stay in
the present. Kids don't need to recollect how things used to be
or how they might be in the future. Concentrate on the here
and now, and on making this a happy experience."

At two o'clock on a December afternoon, the handlers and
their animals, including Buttercup the rabbit, met in the lobby
of the hospital. After Paulette had checked them all, they
walked upstairs to the third floor, where the children were
waiting for the animals to arrive. Some of the patients were in
strollers, some in wheelchairs, and one who had been in a car
accident and was in traction was wheeled in in his bed. Some
children were hooked up to IV poles. Some had no hair. Some

were swathed in bandages. Some were carrying emesis basins. But they all grinned when the dogs came strolling in.

The children petted the dogs, hugged and kissed them, and fed them treats. Children in wheelchairs were given a pull around the room. Candy canes were passed out, and Dave took Polaroid pictures of each child with the dog (or rabbit) of his or her choice. The photos, along with a Good Shepherd necklace and a teddy bear, went to each child as a remembrance of this happy time. The handlers, the children, the hospital personnel, perhaps even the dogs and Buttercup, counted the visit a grand success.

About seven that evening, Lana got a call from the hospital's child-life therapist. "I made a terrible mistake today," he said, "and I'm wondering if I can ask you to help me. A little boy who hasn't much time left was really looking forward to seeing the dogs, but he was asleep when they came and we overlooked bringing him to the recreation room. His mother says Simon has been brave all week, not crying or complaining on the promise of seeing the dogs, but when he found he had missed them, he began to sob. The nurses don't know if he will make it through the night. Do you think someone could possibly come now?"

Lana quickly ran down in her mind which handler might be available, who would have a dog ready, who could deal with a dying boy. "How much time do I have to get someone?"

"Not much. None, really. The boy has been unhooked from the life support systems."

So little time meant Grizzly and she would have to go, Lana realized. But not alone. She would need to have someone with her. She called Bruce Wignal, who had two children of his own. He and Aspen, his golden retriever, were the best team working with children. "Bruce, I've got a special assignment," she said. "This is the situation. Can you make it?"

"Aspen's ready to go," he said. "We can leave in five minutes. What is it you want me to do?"

His own two-year-old had recently been in the hospital. Lana said, "Just do what you would if it were your son."

"Okay, I'll be there."

It had been snowing during the day and now it was icy, but Lana and Grizzly and Bruce and Aspen made it through to the hospital. The child-life therapist met them in the lobby and hustled them to the stairwell and up the stairs; it was against hospital rules for dogs to make a bedside visit, although in this case special permission had been obtained from the head nurse. The therapist led them to the little boy's room and quietly opened the door.

"The dogs are here. Is he . . . ?" The boy's mother nodded and tried to smile. The boy himself had a sheet drawn up to his chin, and his large brown eyes were staring straight ahead.

Lana went to the side of the bed. "Hello, Simon. I have a couple of special friends here who would like to visit with you. This is Grizzly; he's a big German shepherd. Aspen is a golden retriever. Would you like to see them?"

Almost imperceptibly, the boy's head nodded. Lana had Grizzly put his front paws up on the bed and Bruce, at the foot of the bed, had Aspen follow suit. Simon's eyes got even bigger as he stared at the dogs. His mother beamed through the weariness that showed in the deep dark circles under her eyes. "Oh, thank you for coming," she whispered. "Simon has tried all week to be a good boy and not to cry. He knew the dogs were coming and he would get to see them if he didn't cry. Then we found out he'd slept through the visit and it broke his heart. I'm so sorry to bring you out like this."

"We're delighted to be here," Lana said.

And Bruce added, "Thank you for thinking of us."

"Simon," Lana said, "would you like Grizzly to lie beside you so you can pet him?" Again the tiny nod came. "Okay, we need to scoot you over a little bit." Simon's mother helped to move the paper-thin boy and placed a drawsheet on the bed. Grizzly

put his forepaws on the bed, and as Lana lifted his
hindquarters up, he inched his way into position. His body,
longer than the boy's, touched along the boy's length, and he
tucked his nose into the hollow beneath the boy's shoulder.
Simon moved his hand to pet Griz with a touch as light as a
blade of grass moving in a breeze.

A nurse burst into the room. "His vitals are skyrocketing!"

"Oh my gosh, I'm sorry," Lana said. "Do you want the dog
off?"

"No, no, you're okay."

"If Simon just keeps petting him, I'm sure they'll go down,"
Lana said, basing her assurance on the fact that a great deal of
research shows that petting an animal reduces heart rate and
blood pressure. Both the nurse and the boy's mother were
smiling broadly, which struck Lana as weird. She did not know
what move to make, so she suggested to Grizzly that he talk to
Simon, which he did very softly in his throat. Bruce followed
the nurse out of the room to get his gear bag, and when he
came back in, he too was smiling. He put Aspen up on the bed
on the other side of the boy and took Polaroid pictures of the
three, which he gave to Simon. Lana told Simon that whenever
he wanted, he could close his eyes and think of how soft Griz
and Aspen were and how much they liked him. To remind

him, Grizzly and Aspen would leave one of their friends with him, a fuzzy teddy bear, and the bear would sleep with him to keep him company.

The nurses' station with its bank of monitors was right outside the door. "What did we do wrong?" Lana asked when she and Bruce came out of Simon's room with the dogs.

The nurse explained that when Grizzly had gotten up on the bed, the boy's heart rate, his blood pressure, and his respiration rate all shot up to normal. "That's what I meant when I said skyrocketing. They went up to normal!"

The child-life therapist thanked Lana and Bruce over and over as he escorted them down to the lobby. Out in the cold night air, Lana and Bruce said little, their hearts heavy for the boy who would be gone by morning and yet glad because they had been able to give a few moments of happiness and comfort to a dying child and his grieving mother. ❈

A Light from the Manger

SHARI SMYTH

*I*n 1978, we lived on eighteen rolling acres in Pennsylvania. We'd acquired a cow, a few sheep, a horse, and Susie, our wooly nine-hands-high Shetland pony. Susie was past due to give birth. In her stall, her fetlocks deep in fresh straw, she waddled to me, round as a ripe pear. Her big, soft eyes were trusting. It was her first foal. Mine too.

That night I slept in our barn. It was cold and dark and smelled of fresh hay and stale dirt and dusty cobwebs. The cow mooed. The sheep stamped and stirred. I got up and shined a light in Susie's stall, careful not to hit her eyes. She was lying down, looking miserable. She nickered softly. I shuffled back to my pallet and lay down. A growing anxiety gripped me. *What will I do if something goes wrong with the birth?* I tried to pray, but the words wouldn't come.

The next day went by. Nothing. That night I was back in the barn. The cow and sheep were strangely quiet. Moonlight flooded through the open doors. I tiptoed to Susie's stall, and there it was: just born, lying on wet straw, tiny dark hooves flailing out of its birth sack. The new mother gently cleaned her baby with her rough tongue. It was a filly, a girl.

Like a pro, Susie nudged and nickered her filly to its thin, gangly legs. A fuzzy tuft of mane waved over a downy, cinnamon coat. Gumming her way across her mother with squeals and sucking noises, the filly latched on to a nipple.

Leaning on a rough post, I breathed the tart stable air in deep, relieved gulps. I bowed my head and, with sudden clarity, the light of Christmas shone like the stars. It really happened; the majestic, holy Creator was born a baby on a night like this, in a place like this, among His lowly animals, amid straw and dirt and the darkness of our sin. ❄

A Doggie Kind of Christmas

NANCY TOMAZIC

C hristmas was just five days away, and my
daughter and I were busy making Christmas cookies.
Helen was about to turn nine, and she was enthralled
with the idea that she was now old enough to bake real cookies
in a real oven.

We had gone to the store and purchased a variety of cookie
cutters, in all shapes and sizes, from gingerbread men, to
Christmas trees, to Santa in his sleigh. Then we'd loaded a
shopping cart with all the necessary baking supplies. Our
grand plan was to make an enormous assortment of cookies
and use them to decorate our eight-foot-tall Christmas tree.

Helen and I spent three busy, fun-filled days in the kitchen.
The two dogs, Snoopy and Mopsie, our little loveable mutts,
lay by the kitchen door, patiently awaiting the occasional
tidbit we would throw them. They loved cookies more than
anything, and it would have been cruel not to let them have
a taste every now and then.

By the end of the third day, we stood back and proudly
surveyed our masterpieces. There were tiny images of Santa
dressed in red with plush white trim, Rudolph with his very
red nose, Christmas trees adorned with colorful decorations,

and tiny packages wrapped with colorful ribbons. Eagerly, we strung them with silk ribbons and hung them about the Christmas tree. Son John, who was older, climbed the ladder and placed a bright, glistening cookie-star at the very top.

By ten o'clock that night, the tree was beautifully decorated, and the three of us reveled in the sight of our very special Christmas tree. We had promised ourselves that on Christmas morning, we would eat some of the delicious-looking cookies, but until then they would adorn the tree. Tomorrow night would be Christmas Eve, and we would have a houseful of relatives. The kids seemed more excited about showing off their tree than opening their much-anticipated gifts.

By six o'clock on Christmas Eve, our living room was full of loved ones, ranging in age from three to ninety. The kids and I had been busy all day, they helping to clean the house while I cooked a vast array of holiday dishes. Now Christmas music floated above the cheerful voices of our relatives. The Christmas tree stood proudly in front of the front window, its colorful lights ablaze and highlighting our workmanship. The children beamed with pride as everyone complimented them on their exquisite tree. A mountain of presents surrounded the tree, placed there by relatives who would share in the joy of the holidays.

Everyone took turns opening his or her gifts. Soon there were piles of clothing toys, kitchen gadgets and all else distributed about the room, and only two gifts remained under the tree. One was for Snoopy and one for Mopsie. Helen placed the presents in front of the dogs, and they began to playfully tear away the wrappings. Snoopy's gift was a packet of miniature dog biscuits, her favorite brand. Within a few minutes, I knew Snoopy would have the biscuits devoured. Mopsie received a large rawhide dog bone, which was his favorite chew toy. But to my surprise, once the dogs had opened their gifts, they left them where they lay and retreated to a far corner of the living room. "Well," I thought, "perhaps they don't like all the noise and commotion." I gathered their gifts up and set them by their respective dog dishes. Once things quieted down, they would be able to enjoy them.

By midnight, the last of our relatives were donning their coats and preparing to depart. It had been a very special evening, and a Christmas Eve my children were sure to remember. We were saying good-bye to Aunt June and Uncle Bob, two of our favorite relatives. Uncle Bob was a very quiet person who spoke softly but whose eyes always showed a hint of mischief. Aunt June stepped out in the snow, and Uncle Bob began to follow. Then he stopped and turned toward me.

"I have to ask you something," he said. "Why aren't there any cookies on the lower part of your tree?" His eyes were sparkling mischievously.

Confused, I looked back at our Christmas tree. Yep, there sure weren't any cookies on the lower part of the tree.

"Oh *nooo*!" I cried. "Mopsie! Snoopy!" The two dogs were lying huddled in the far corner, slothful expressions on both of their faces. They seemed overly content.

"No wonder they didn't want their Christmas presents!" I said, and then began to laugh.

"Well, I guess we aren't the only ones who overate around here." Uncle Bob laughed, and gave me a departing hug. "Just wondered," he said, smiling. "I guess everyone had a good Christmas."

On Christmas morning, John got the ladder out and handed down a selection of Christmas cookies for us to enjoy. "Boy, Mom," Helen said, "I'm sure glad our dogs aren't any bigger, or we wouldn't have *any* cookies to eat!"

It had been a special Christmas for everyone, dogs included. ❄

Luther

MICHELLE WHEELER CULMORE

AS TOLD TO

JOE L. WHEELER

wo Christmases ago, my daughter Michelle first told me the story of Luther. It is a story that has refused to go away. We humans are so glib about the taking of a life. Not just human life, but animal and bird as well. But the Creator, in His great wisdom, put each one of them on this planet for a reason. A reason my daughter now understands.

I tried, in its retelling, to preserve the natural rhythm of my daughter's original narrative. It is told simply, naturally, just as she remembers it.

Actually, it was a miracle that I ever met Luther, because he had been bought earlier in the fall to fatten up for Thanksgiving dinner. But something happened along the way to give him a Hezekiah reprieve: they fell in love with him— to have eaten him would have been like eating one of the family!

So partly, at least, to get him out of temptation's way, he was delivered to the theater to begin his dramatic career.

A senior fashion major, I was interning in a New England public theater, cutting my teeth—and other body parts—on costume design and repair.

Having always yearned to be in New England in the fall—
and in the winter—the opportunity seemed almost too good to
be true. When I arrived, it was to the lazy, hazy days of late
summer when the heat slows life down to a catlike slouch. But
before long, the cooler winds of autumn swept down from
Canada, and all nature came alive again.

Soon it was "peak," as the natives label it, and all across New
England the leaves turned to scarlet, orange, amber and gold.
Their reflection in the sky blue of the lakes and rivers took
one's breath away. And spearing through the rainbow of colors
were the soaring spires of blinding white churches, legacy of
those intrepid Puritans three and three-quarter centuries ago.

And then came Luther.

They sent him to stay at the theater for the remainder of the
fall season. He came with his snow-white feathers and in a
small cage with some plain, dried food and a water dish. Not
knowing what else to do with him, they hauled him down to
the theater basement with the unwarranted assumption that
the stage manager Torsten would somehow take care
of him.

The theater basement was one of the places I hated the most.
It was very, very, *very* dirty, damp, dark and unorganized. I
can't even *begin* to describe how dirty it was. Sort of a dumping

ground for the theater: stage supplies, props, tools, trash and remnants of the theater itself were strewn all over. And like most New England buildings, it had been there a long, long time. It was even said that there was a resident ghost. If true, it surely slept a lot, because no one I knew had ever seen it. Nor had I.

The basement was under the theater itself but was not paved or floored. It was essentially gravel, rocks, loose rusty nails, cement chunks and who knows what else. One never went down there without heavy shoes on. When I remembered—and could find one—I'd wear a mask. Heaven only knows what toxic chemicals (asbestos, etc.) were staining the air—and it was grossly filthy to boot. Every time I went down, within an hour or so, I'd get a headache, feel like I was coming down with a cold, and get a runny nose. And the grime in the air would rain down on body and clothes; in no time at all, I was filthy—inside and out.

I have to give Torsten credit, however. He did his best to fix it up during those rare occasions when he had spare time. As foul as it was, it was said to be an improvement on his predecessor's subterranean junkyard, one stratum down.

Needless to say, imagine what all this did to the beautiful, clean goose—stuck down there for more than a month! In no

time at all, he had lost his shimmering white beauty and had
turned an ugly, grimy gray. And his health obviously suffered
as well.

As if these conditions and the intermittent darkness were
not enough, there were the kids—all 150 of them—streaming
downstairs in hordes to be measured for their *Christmas Carol*
costuming. They needed that many because there were two
children's casts and a month-long run; out of the hundred and
fifty, they hoped fifty a night would actually
show up.

Unfortunately, we could only process them a few at a
time—and that left the others with time on their hands. To no
one's surprise, they didn't wait well. In fact, it was bedlam! Just
the memory of it gives me a headache.

Worse yet, it didn't take them long to discover Luther. They
took turns playing with him, teasing him, taunting him,
mistreating him. Amazingly, not once did he use that sharp
beak of his to strike back. He just took it.

The staff wasn't much help, either. Quite frankly, they were
ticked that this unexpected responsibility had been thrust
upon them. A not unsurprising response, given the fact that
they were all overworked and underpaid—if paid at all.

So . . . Luther honked and pooped (green, by the way) all the time—most likely because he was in goose hell and yearned to get out.

I suppose he became attached to me because I was the one around the most and consequently paid the most attention to him. I ended up being the one who fed and watered him most of the time. At that time, we were in the concluding days of *Othello* and frantically—almost simultaneously, of course!—preparing for *A Christmas Carol*.

Luther detested his cage and used his canny mind to the fullest in figuring out ways to ditch it. As a result, he got out often. And when he didn't get out on his own, the kids *helped*! During one of these escapes, he cut one of his webbed feet on a rusty nail. Fortunately, Tracey (one of the actresses) had previously worked for a veterinarian. She was the only one (other than me, and later on, Jay—head costumer and actor) sympathetic to Luther's plight.

We dug up some first aid stuff and tried to clean up his poor foot—no easy task when the grimy sink appears to never have been washed itself. Nothing was clean down there to ever set such a precedent! Then, we put him in the shower (disgustingly dirty, too, but the "cleanest" alternative around), and Tracey, costume, stage makeup and all, got in with him. I locked the bathroom door (to keep kids and others out) and joined her in the cleaning process.

Unfortunately, she forgot she was supposed to go on stage when she was "called," nor was I there to help with last-minute costume changes and alterations, etc. The play went on without us (luckily for her, in that scene she was only an extra). But as I'll describe later on, the director added a scene not in the script when he tracked us down after the curtain call.

Anyway, we used soap and shampoo to clean Luther up, feather by feather, layer by layer. He adjusted to this tripartite shower with such nonchalance one would have thought such strange doings were part of his normal routine. We were a little apprehensive about what effect shampoo might have on the natural oil in his feathers but concluded that few alternatives were worse than his current state. We then toweled him off (a process that gradually revealed light gray feathers); cleaned, disinfected, wrapped up his foot as best we could, and taped it; and he was free to try to walk. He was very cheerful about it—except for the dubious looks he gave our bandaging artistry—and began cleaning his feathers.

The next morning, he was white again.

And so Luther and I became friends.

Once he got to know me, he adored my petting him. He was most inquisitive, always wanting to know what was going on. Had he been a cat, he would have been purring on my lap; being a goose, he took second best and enthroned himself on the floor beneath my sewing machine.

And he was *very* vocal. I'd love to have a transcript decoding his end of our long talks together.

The bandage kept coming off—or snipped off, we never knew which—but we tried to monitor his recovery as best we could. He'd get dirty again and again and again. I tried to keep him with me as much as possible, but it was difficult—and more than a little annoying—as what went in one end promptly came out the other. In a steady stream. He never seemed to feel the need to wait for a "more convenient season"; consequently I was continually cleaning up behind him, feeling much like a circus lady with a shovel in the wake of an elephant. Disgusting! Nevertheless, the process didn't seem to humiliate *him*! He followed me around everywhere I went in those downstairs catacombs, honking indignantly as if to say, "Hey! Where do you think you're going? Wait up!"

As the *Christmas Carol* marathon began gathering speed and my work accelerated at an ever-faster pace, I moved my ironing

board, sewing machine and so on over to the theater basement
and into the backstage makeup room. Luther thought he had
died and gone to heaven when I moved him in, too, to keep me
company. Maintaining sideways eye contact (goose fashion),
he honked away with his stories hour after hour, only stopping
once in a while to take a nap.

Then, as we neared zero hour, I worked there with Luther
virtually around the clock, till I was hard-pressed to avoid
falling asleep at my sewing machine. Every once in a while,
I'd shake myself awake again, only to look down and
see Luther eyeing me with puzzled concern and honking
solace.

Opening night came at last, but this time I was almost too
tired to care. Everyone else, however, was illuminated by that
inner excitement that always accompanies first-night
performances. Rumor was that a big-time city critic was going
to be there, which added an extra edge to the excitement.

Soon I could hear the crowd upstairs. The milling around.
The voices. And the clapping. And after all the work I had
done, I wasn't even able to sit back in the auditorium and enjoy
seeing my handiwork. I was still sewing, still altering, still
helping to salvage or repair garments during and after each

scene. Before the winter street scenes, it was a madhouse putting mittens, hats, coats and mufflers on all the fidgety children before their entrances onstage. As an added treat, just before the biggest scene, one frightened little girl, overwhelmed by stage fright, threw up on half-a-dozen costumes we had spent so much time mending, cleaning and ironing. This created an even madder rush to find costumes to replace them.

And then it was finally time for the big street scene, when Dickens' London was reproduced in all its vitality and diversity: with fifty children—all behaving now, wide-eyed and innocent—with several pet dogs and a pet ferret (one previous year, there had been a horse!). The entire cast was onstage at the same time . . . and Luther.

Not long before Tiny Tim's piping "God bless us. Every one!" would bring that beloved story full circle, Luther had celebrated his acting debut by waddling across the stage. Noting how frightened he looked, Jay leaned down and picked him up, tenderly cradling his feathered (white again) body in his arms and feeling the tom-tom of his fast-beating heart. From that refuge, Luther contentedly looked out over the delighted audience and honked out a soft "Hello."

Sadly, I was not able to stay for the rest of the run. In all my last-minute packing and bequeathing of responsibilities, however, one worry remained constant: *After I am gone, what will happen to poor Luther?* We moved his cage to a far corner of the basement (actually, into Torsten's office). There was thus a cement floor and a door we could shut (1) to try to keep the kids from tormenting him and (2) to keep his lonely squawks from disturbing the audience. This room was much, much better than the first. But there he was, left alone. I felt terribly guilty every time I shut that door and heard him entreating me to come back.

As the last moments of my tenure at the theater passed, Luther began squawking nonstop. Actually "squawking" is a totally inadequate word for what I heard. No one word in the dictionary can begin to capture it; the closest I can come to is that it was halfway between an outraged squawk and a heartbroken sob. There was absolutely no question in my mind: he *knew*! Even though Jay promised to take care of him, I knew it would never be the same. It was heart-wrenching. It was terrible!

I still hear him . . . in sleepless nights . . . in restless days . . . How this one little goose—nothing but soiled once-white feathers, two inquisitive eyes, a honking story that never quite got told, and a heart as big as all New England—could make such a difference in this hectic life I live, I guess I'll never understand. It just has.

That Christmas, Jay, bless him!—knowing I'm such a sentimental ol' fool—sent me a present. It was small, and my fingers shook a little as I opened it. It was a lovely ceramic ornament. One side was flat. But the other side featured, in relief, a white bird. A goose. Luther! ❅

A Dog Named Bandit

RONALD "SCOTTY" BOURNE

or many years I have been placing a little figure of a dog next to the infant Jesus in my Nativity set at Christmas. Some people raise their eyebrows, but when they hear my story, they feel differently. For it represents a real dog named Bandit. Whether he belongs there, you judge for yourself.

I got Bandit in 1967 when I was working as an animal trainer for Walt Disney Productions. We were filming *Three without Fear*, a TV movie about three children and a dog trekking across a desert. We needed an animal that looked like a starved Mexican street dog.

At an animal shelter in Glendale, I found a part German shepherd. His ribs protruding through his mangy black-and-gray fur, he fit the part. "Bandit" was what local children had called him for stealing food.

Bandit turned out to be a natural actor. He took direction well and was always ready to play. Sometimes the play got out of hand. When we were filming near Scammon's Lagoon in Mexico, someone threw a stick into the ocean for him to retrieve. A strong undertow carried him along the shore. As he struggled to keep his nose above water, I raced along the high sandbank, trying to reach him before he was carried out to sea. At the last second, I managed to grab his collar and pull him to safety.

Another time, in Arizona, a little raccoonlike animal called a coatimundi, which was appearing in a scene with him, bit Bandit's leg. The animal's razor-sharp teeth severed an artery, and two crew members and I made a mad dash by car sixty miles across the desert to a Tucson veterinarian. As I held Bandit in my arms, I realized how much my friend meant to me. Thank God, a fine vet helped pull Bandit through. I decided then it was time he retired from the movies.

For a while Bandit lived with my sister's family in Simi Valley. He thrived on domestic life and became a neighborhood hero: As his movies appeared on television, there was a constant demand for him to "speak," "shake hands" and pose for pictures. Bandit loved the attention and had infinite patience.

Moreover, he had an almost human understanding of people's needs. For example, one of my sister's boys was born with splayed feet. The doctor prescribed braces and told her not to expect the child to walk at the normal time. However, one day, to everyone's surprise, Bandit was seen walking very slowly across the yard with the baby toddling behind, hanging onto the dog's bushy tail!

Then came a time when everything in my life fell apart. After a broken romance, I was at my lowest ebb. Bandit and I got back together again, and during long reflective walks on the beach, he was my only companion. Though now graying at his muzzle, he still wanted me to throw a ball and play with him. This was my therapy, for Bandit coaxed me out of my melancholy solitude.

As my outlook improved, I deepened my relationship with the Lord. This led me into many new areas, one of which was a juvenile prison ministry. Bandit accompanied me on my visits to the teenage boys; they loved to hear his story, especially about my finding him in "prison."

However, by 1979 Bandit was old and painfully stiff; I sensed it would be his last Christmas, and I asked the Lord to help me make it especially significant, not only because of Bandit, but because of my new life with God.

By mid-December I was afraid Bandit would not even make it to Christmas. One day while praying over him, I envisioned myself going to the stable at Bethlehem. Carrying my old friend in my arms, I presented him to the infant Jesus. I explained to Jesus that my gift was the only treasure I had left.

Slowly, I placed Bandit beside the baby Jesus and then turned and walked away.

The picture I had while praying became a reality on Christmas Eve. Bandit lay on the lawn, unable to stand. His brown eyes, glazed with pain, looked up at me imploringly. In anguish I called the animal shelter, and I placed Bandit in my car for the last time. The man at the shelter took him gently, and I stood waiting outside until he brought me Bandit's collar; he put his hand on my shoulder and told me it was all over.

All the way home I begged, "Lord, I know he was just a dog, but he meant the world to me and I loved him. Please let me know if he is with you."

I was still grieving the next morning as I arrived at the detention camp to conduct a Christmas communion service. I really didn't feel like being there. The boys were at a low point too, for they had nothing to give their families, who would be visiting later in the day. Our service was held in a small television room, the only decoration being a simple Nativity set on the table that served as an altar.

As I talked to the boys about the spirit of giving, I said, "People place too much emphasis on expensive gifts. The greatest gift you can give is what you seem to place the least value on. While we're taking communion, I suggest each of you offer Jesus the one precious gift that no one else can give: yourself."

When it was over, as the boys started filing out the door, I happened to look down at the manger scene. I stared transfixed. Standing beside the crib of the baby Jesus was a little statue of a dog. A dog that looked like Bandit—in the exact spot where I had placed him in my prayer.

With a tight throat, I asked, "Who—where did the dog come from?" The boys all shook their heads.

No one at the center had any idea who put the small figure of a dog there or where it came from. So I gently put the figure in my pocket, looked up and silently thanked God for answering my prayer. ✲

A Parrot Taught Me Her Song

RONALD L. HARMON

*S*hortly after my mother passed away, my father was diagnosed with congestive heart failure. For ten years I helped my father, and every waking moment became filled with caregiving on top of a full-time job. It was difficult for me to give so much, but love for my father motivated me to do everything I could.

After Dad died I felt alone, as if my days couldn't get any darker. Although I soon realized a freedom I'd never experienced during all the years of helping my father, this was tempered by the fact that because I'd spent so much time caring for someone, my life took on a chilling sort of emptiness.

Friends suggested I get a pet. I thought about the idea but didn't have a clue what kind of animal best suited me. A friend from Germany visited my home after staying with a family in Canada. He kept telling me about the clever little bird his Canadian hosts had. Having a bird in the house began to sound wonderful. My friend assured me that birds are clean and easy to care for. He tried hard to convince me that I should consider getting a bird companion. But a married couple I knew had a parrot whose loud screams made me nervous when I visited them, and I knew this sort of pet wouldn't work for me. I thought about the pros and cons of dogs, cats and even guinea pigs, but I decided a bird just didn't seem to be in my future.

One afternoon I went to a local shopping center and ambled into the pet store. Perched in the open near the front door sat an exquisite soft gray parrot with a red tail. A couple of customers commented about how tame the little feathered creature seemed when she allowed them to stroke her head. Suddenly, I found myself thinking, *I want this bird.* Immediately, though, I squelched the idea of buying a pet and left the store.

The image of the little gray bird stayed with me as my car seemed to float down the highway away from the store. Even names for the new pet drifted through my mind. After some thought, I settled on calling the bird Buddy. I'd driven about a mile or two along the highway when I decided to go back and buy Buddy, no matter what the cost. That day began a relationship like none I'd ever thought could be possible with an animal.

As if in answer to my pre-Buddy loneliness, the bird liked to whistle for me when I left the room, never wanting me to be out of her sight for too long. If I didn't answer Buddy's whistle soon enough, she'd come looking for me. When friends dropped in, Buddy would climb down the ladder from the top of her cage to see who had stopped by. The minute my guests saw the little parrot, she became the center of attention. My friends and I would sit on the floor and play with Buddy and she'd happily hop from one person to another, lifting her foot to be picked up or performing some other trick to get our attention.

One of my favorite experiences with Buddy was how she responded to having me read stories to her while she was still too young to talk. Some nights I read stories, substituting Buddy's name for one of the characters. She seemed thrilled and listened with childlike interest. Winter nights often felt cold and dark when I got off work, but because of Buddy, my little house loomed cozy and warm. The thought of this happy little bird being there filled my heart with gratitude. In the evenings I'd sit in the television room with Buddy perched nearby on a wooden hall tree. Together we'd watch television or listen to music in comfortable companionship.

When Christmas inched closer, I thought it would be difficult and sad with my family gone. One comfort was that Buddy and I would be celebrating the young parrot's first Christmas together. As the cold winter mornings edged their way to Christmas, my little friend would sit on top of her cage and sing as if thanking God for being alive. It surprised me when some of the Christmas carols became Buddy's favorites and she'd sing along to them. Buddy in her own way added something special that only she could bring to the spirit of Christmas, and I loved her for it.

Buddy was four months old when we began sharing our lives together. When I first saw the lovely African grey at the pet store, I didn't know it, but Buddy was destined to fill a void in my existence. Because of my relationship with Buddy, I no longer was lonely but experienced a true expression of God's love. Buddy's companionship gives me the lasting gifts that make every day Christmas. ❄

A Blue Christmas

Starla "Misty" Spray

*L*ectures. Term papers. Finals. Grades. College was nothing but pressure on top of pressure. I was carrying a full course load at Bauder in Arlington, Texas, the fall semester of my sophomore year and feeling like I had a weight the size of the Lone Star State on my shoulders. The fact that it was Friday didn't matter one bit. I was looking at a weekend of studying. I wondered where I would find time even for church on Sunday. I drove my usual route home to my parents' and hoped the familiar sights along the way would ease my stress. But the big old weeping willow I'd watched grow from a skinny sapling, my high school alma mater, the garland-wrapped streetlights downtown—that day they didn't do a thing for me.

I turned onto North Center Street and drove by the lawn with the big plastic Nativity figures. The crib was empty, and the light in the cow had burned out. I slowed the car while some tall boys moved their football game out of the street. Up ahead was the weather-beaten two-story house that always stuck in my mind. The paint was chipped and peeling, the steps to the front porch sagged, and I imagined big empty rooms inside. The frail old man who lived there was sitting out front, as usual, his black Lab lying lazily in the tall grass at his feet. *He's got his Bible out again*, I noted. Once I'd heard him reciting passages to the dog! A couple times I'd felt the urge to stop and say hi, just talk to him for a few minutes, see if he was all right, but I was always too busy. I glanced in my rearview mirror. "Reading the Bible to a dog," I murmured, hitting the brakes. "How lonely can a person get?"

In the next open driveway I turned the car around, breaking up the boys' ball game again. I parked in front of the run-down house and got out of my car. "Hi," I called to the old man, suddenly feeling awkward. "Nice day, isn't it?"

"Come on and sit awhile," he said, scooting over on the steps to make room for me. "I'm Diggs," he said, "and that's my dog Blue."

Mr. Diggs smiled. "Mostly I read the Bible. I have plenty of time for reading these days."

"You live alone?" I asked.

"I wouldn't put it that way exactly," Mr. Diggs said. "My wife and most of my friends are gone from this world, but I'm never alone. Not as long as I have my faith." Blue let loose an expressive whine and nosed Mr. Diggs's shoe. "Yes, yes, boy," he laughed, "and I've got you too. But that goes without saying." He leaned over to rub Blue's back, and I saw how much he loved him.

"Blue likes to listen to me read," Mr. Diggs said. "You have time for a story, Misty?"

"Maybe just one," I said, getting a little nervous about everything I had to do.

The old man turned to the story of the first Christmas in Luke. *I hope this doesn't take too long*, I thought. Blue rested his chin on his crossed paws as if pleased to sit and listen all day. I scratched my knee and tried to sneak a peek at my watch.

"'Behold,'" Mr. Diggs read, slowing down as he repeated the angel's holy announcement, "'I bring you good tidings of great joy . . .'"

Christmas had always been a joyful time for me too, but that year it had taken a backseat to school. Everything had. I stayed quiet, though, till Mr. Diggs finished. When he had, part of me was sorry. He had a way about him that was calming, and while he was reading, his voice a little like a good preacher's, I'd almost forgotten my worries. "I'd better get going," I said. "My parents will be holding dinner, and I have loads of schoolwork."

Mr. Diggs invited me back anytime. "Old Blue and I will be here. You can count on that."

I said I'd stop by again, but pretty quick I fell back into my routine of studying, studying and more studying, and worrying about studying in between. On the day before school let out for Christmas break, I drove down North Center Street again. Mr. Diggs was there on the porch, head in his hands. Something was wrong. I stretched my neck to look into the tall grass. Blue! He was gone! No way could I stop. What would I say? I sped by. At home I threw myself onto my bed, feeling guilty.

When I refused my mom's meatloaf and mashed potatoes, she figured I had a flu bug. I knew different. I was sick of myself. It was time to get my nose out of my books and do something that wasn't about me.

On Christmas Eve I drove the familiar route toward school. I didn't have class; Mom had said I could invite Mr. Diggs over for Christmas dinner. I turned down North Center Street, passed the big Nativity scene and parked in front of the old house. *Why isn't he outside on a nice day like this?* I wondered, walking up to the porch. I knocked hard on the door and heard shuffling footsteps inside. Mr. Diggs pulled open the door and smiled. "Come on in, Misty," he said. "What a surprise."

I stepped inside, and when he closed the door the house fell quiet. Blue was nowhere to be seen, except in pictures scattered all around the den. There were other pictures too, of Mr. Diggs and his wife, waving from a ship, sharing a beach umbrella, sitting at a tiny table in a fancy restaurant. But mostly there were pictures of Blue. Mr. Diggs saw me staring at the one of Blue swimming with a big stick in his mouth. "He played fetch in the gulf for two solid hours that day," he remembered. "There was a bit of an undertow, but Blue was a mighty strong swimmer."

Was? I looked at Mr. Diggs.

"Blue's disappeared," he said, his voice shaky. "I can't hardly sit out on the porch these days. It makes me miss him all the more."

"I'm sorry, Mr. Diggs. Really I am. Your wife, your friends . . . now Blue." I began to cry. He'd lost everything.

Mr. Diggs handed me his hankie. "Don't forget, Misty, I've got my faith. That's the constant in my life. Hard as they may be, the rough patches pass. I've prayed for Blue to come home, and now it's up to the Lord."

I sniffled. "But what if Blue doesn't come back . . . ever?"

"He's in the Lord's capable hands. So am I. So are you too, Misty." I was amazed that even now he was ready to accept whatever God had in store.

"Do you believe in Christmas?" Mr. Diggs asked. "In the promise of Jesus' birth? God never leaves us. No matter what else may be happening in our lives, happy or sad, Christmas is coming. And Christmas always comes, Misty. You can count on that."

I dried my eyes. "That's why I stopped by, actually. To invite you to spend tomorrow with my family." Mr. Diggs accepted, and I raced home to tell Mom to set the extra place at our table.

When I arrived on Christmas Day to pick him up, Mr. Diggs was wearing an old gray suit and a tad too much aftershave. He offered his arm and escorted me to my car. As he held open my door I noticed something in the distance: a parade of children coming up the street. I recognized the tall boys whose football game I'd disrupted. Younger kids led the pack. A black spot next to one of the kids started to take shape as they moved toward us. Could it be?

"Blue!" Mr. Diggs shouted, and his friend came running. The kids caught up and gathered around us, telling how they'd seen the dog several blocks away and knew he belonged on North Center Street. We all petted Blue and welcomed him home. "How 'bout taking a nap till I get back?" Mr. Diggs said. Blue circled a few times and then lay down in his spot in the tall grass. The neighborhood kids promised to keep an eye on him while they played outside with their new bikes and roller skates.

Mr. Diggs waved to them as we drove down North Center Street past the lawn with the big Nativity. The baby lay in the manger, and the light in the cow had been replaced. "See what I told you, Misty?" Mr. Diggs said. "Christmas always comes."

We enjoyed our day together, and when I brought Mr. Diggs home, Blue was there waiting.

Driving to school the first day classes resumed, I saw the old man at his usual post. This time, though, Blue wasn't the sole audience for his Bible reading. At Mr. Diggs's feet were nine or ten kids from the neighborhood. I honked and waved. College wasn't going to get any easier, but the rough patches would pass. And after all, Christmas was only a few hundred days away. ❄

The Undersea Reindeer

ALLAN ZULLO

*A*s his submarine docked for repairs at the harbor of Polyarny in the far northwest corner of the Soviet Union, Commander Geoffrey Sladen stood on the bridge and buttoned the collar of his coat.

It was a cold, blustery, overcast day in 1941—one that reminded him of winter in London, where he wished he could be right now. He worried about his wife Sarah and their three children, and wondered how they were coping without him in the war-ravaged country.

As commander of H.M.S. *Trident*, he had been at sea for nearly six months and missed his family terribly. But Great Britain was fighting for its life against Germany as World War II entered its third year, and he had a job to do.

Sladen's vessel was part of a fleet of British submarines defending merchant ships that carried badly needed supplies to the Soviet Union, an important ally of Great Britain. The *Trident* also patrolled the seas off the Norwegian coast, hunting for German ships to torpedo. During one sea battle, the submarine sank an enemy supply ship but suffered damage to one of its engines from the blast of a German depth charge.

The sub made it safely to Polyarny, where repairs were expected to take about a week. From the vessel's bridge, Sladen allowed himself a moment to forget about the war and daydream about his loving family.

If I do nothing else on shore leave, he thought, *I must get Sarah something nice for Christmas.* It was only October, but Sladen liked to plan ahead. He thought about getting her authentic wooden Russian Easter eggs—delicately painted faces and scenes on egg-shaped wood with a shiny lacquer finish. *Maybe she would like a porcelain animal figure or a blown-glass vase.*

But Sladen never got the chance to shop. He was too busy overseeing the repair work and plotting strategy with Soviet navy officials, especially Admiral Vladimir Petrovich. The two developed a quick friendship, and on the night before the *Trident* was to head out to sea, Sladen accepted the admiral's invitation to dinner at the Russian's home.

They talked mostly about the war, of course, but during the meal, the subject of Christmas came up.

"It is my most favorite time of year," said Sladen. "I have such great memories as a child, waiting for the arrival of Father Christmas. And now that I have young children of my own, I read them an American poem called 'A Visit from Saint

Nicolas.'" The commander closed his eyes, smiled, and recited a passage from that classic poem:

> "With a little old driver so lively and quick,
> I knew in a moment it must be Saint Nick.
> More rapid than eagles, his coursers they came,
> And he whistled and shouted and called them by name:
> 'Now, Dasher! Now, Dancer! Now, Prancer and Vixen!
> On, Comet! On, Cupid! On, Donner and Blitzen!
> To the top of the porch! To the top of the wall!
> Now dash away! Dash away! Dash away all!'"

Petrovich applauded Sladen and joined him in a hearty laugh.

"We have our own Saint Nick or, as you call him, Father Christmas," said the admiral. "Here in the Soviet Union, we call him Ded Moroz. That translates in English to Grandfather Frost. He brings presents to children. However, unlike Father Christmas arriving at children's homes in a flying sleigh, Grandfather Frost brings the gifts in person. And he comes on New Year's Day, not Christmas day. It is a wonderful time. Families gather around the *yolka* and . . . "

"What's that?" asked Sladen. "A giant egg yolk?"

Petrovich chuckled. "A *yolka* is our version of a Christmas tree decorated with homemade ornaments and fruit and candy. Sometimes, for the small children, Grandfather Frost places gifts under the New Year tree with the help of Snegurochka, his granddaughter. She's better known as the Snow Maiden. She's dressed in white fur and is beautiful."

"What does Grandfather Frost look like?" Sladen asked.

"He has a long white beard. He wears a fur-lined blue coat and matching hat and big black boots. He walks with a long magical staff and rides in a *troika.* That's a sled drawn by three horses."

Petrovich pointed to the bowl in front of Sladen. "In our house, we make a big pot of *kutya,* which is what you're eating right now."

"It's very good," said the commander, after taking a big sip from his spoon. "It's like a vegetarian porridge."

"That's exactly what it is. My cook has put various types of wheat and grain in it and sweetened it with honey."

With a sly grin, Petrovich said, "Here's what we do on Christmas Eve when we eat *kutya*." To Sladen's stunned amazement, the admiral flung a spoonful of *kutya* toward the ceiling. A big gob stuck on a wooden beam above the table.

"Aha!" Petrovich beamed. "The *kutya* sticks. That's a good omen for the future. Perhaps it means we will win this awful war."

Sladen eyed the glob, calculating in his head exactly where the blob of porridge would land when it peeled off the beam. *I think it will fall into the bowl of boiled potatoes.*

"Go ahead," urged the admiral. "Try it."

"Oh, I couldn't."

"I insist. It's tradition."

"Well, okay." Feeling like a schoolboy about to fire a spitball across the classroom, Sladen scooped a hefty spoonful of *kutya*. Whipping his arm in an underhand motion, he sent the goop flying past the beam and watched it splatter on the ceiling. "It's holding!"

"Bravo, Commander! We are sure to win the war now!"

The dinner conversation returned to more serious matters as the two consumed *kutya*, salted herring, pickled cucumbers, potatoes and fried sturgeon.

At the end of the meal, Petrovich said, "I hope you don't mind that we ate no meat."

"That's perfectly fine, Admiral. I enjoyed the food immensely and am so grateful for your hospitality."

"In my country, I am considered strange. I think in your country I would be called a nutter, a crazy person. I eat seafood and fowl, but I can't bring myself to consume red meat of any kind. That is unusual because I own a small reindeer farm. I sell reindeer milk, but I will not sell a reindeer to be slaughtered for its food or hide or antlers. I will sell them only to people who will use them to pull sleighs or to get milk.

"In the Soviet Union, most reindeer are treated like cattle. They are allowed to graze, and then they are slaughtered. I get laughed at by my fellow officers because I won't kill reindeer. They think I am getting soft. They don't respect reindeer the way you do in Great Britain." He grinned. "At least, you have them flying through the air and pulling Father Christmas's sleigh."

"Yes, reindeer are looked at favorably in my country," said Sladen. "In fact, when Christmas comes, no one would dare hurt a reindeer. They are an important part of the holiday. My children even know the personalities of Father Christmas's reindeer. Dasher is the speediest and Dancer the most graceful. Prancer is the most powerful, while Vixen is the prettiest. Comet brings children wonder and Cupid brings love. As for

Donner and Blitzen, they are pretty rowdy and known as thunder and lightning."

Just then, the glob of *kutya* that Sladen had tossed to the ceiling came loose and splashed right into his glass of wine.

"Ha! Ha! A direct hit," Petrovich chortled.

"Let's hope that's an omen for the *Trident*'s torpedoes," said Sladen. "I would love to score some direct hits on the German ships."

Getting up from the table, the admiral said, "Come, let us sit by the fire. Your children, you have pictures of them?"

Sladen flipped open his billfold and pulled out a photo of his three children—George, seven; Amanda, five; and Elizabeth, one.

"Such handsome children," marveled Petrovich. "Alas, I have none of my own."

"And here is a photo of my wife Sarah," said Sladen. "She and our children live with her parents on a small farm near Scotland, away—I hope—from any bombing. The children love the animals so much. My family likes living there, although it's a little more icy and snowy than in London. Last winter, when Elizabeth was born, Sarah had a nasty time trying to push the pram in all the snow."

As Sladen talked about his family, the admiral seemed in deep thought for a few seconds before a twinkle came to his eyes. A moment later, he changed the subject. "When do you expect to return to your home port?"

"In two weeks. We will be cruising off the Norwegian coast on our way back, looking to attack any German ships in the area."

After a final toast for the success of the Allies, Sladen got up to leave. "Admiral, I can't begin to tell you what a wonderful time I had tonight. The food and company were terrific. I enjoyed talking about Christmas traditions, too, although I confess it made me feel a little homesick."

"May you have a safe voyage home—and sink a few German ships along the way."

The next morning, the commander was aboard the *Trident* going over the latest orders from the Royal Navy with his officers. Meanwhile, crewmen were loading the last of the supplies for the trip home. Sladen paid no attention to the five-foot-by-four-foot wooden crate that was carried aboard by two Russian sailors.

Hours later, the sub slipped away from Polyarny and into the icy gray waters of the Barents Sea. It headed past the northern tip of Finland and toward the western coast of Norway.

"Captain," said first mate Scotty Williams. "We have a crate in the supply room that's making a weird noise."

"What kind of weird noise?" asked Sladen.

"Thumping and whinnying, sir."

"So why haven't you opened it up?"

"Well, sir, the crate is addressed to you personally."

"To me? I didn't order anything."

Sladen followed Williams to the supply room and studied the crate, which had several tiny holes. An unpleasant odor was coming out of them.

"Open it up. Hurry," Sladen ordered, his curiosity heightened.

Williams and another crewman used a crowbar and opened the front of the crate. Their jaws dropped in astonishment when they looked inside.

"What the . . . ?"

"Blimey!"

"What in the world is that?"

From inside peeked two big brown eyes, one on each side of a long, dark gray snout. Triangular-shaped ears were bent sideways on a gray head that was cocked to the side. Beanpolelike legs held up a slender, fuzzy body.

"I don't believe this," Sladen muttered. "It's a baby reindeer!"

On the other side of the crate was taped an envelope addressed to the commander. He opened it up and read the note: "Father Christmas has his reindeer, and now you and your family shall have one too. It will make pushing your pram easier in the snow. Cheers and a happy Christmas. Vladimir."

Sladen had always been cool under fire and had a reputation for making snap decisions. But this time he was speechless.

"Captain, what are we going to do with it?" asked Williams. "Can we butcher it, cook it, and eat it?"

Sladen glared at him. "No, of course not. We'll keep it."

"Begging your pardon, sir. But it's a reindeer . . . on a submarine. Doesn't that sound a little . . . I don't know . . . *bizarre*?"

"It's a Christmas gift. We will keep it as our mascot until we get back to port. The reindeer will be with us for only a couple of weeks."

Accompanying the crate was a smaller box that contained moss, lichen and grass for the animal to eat on its journey to Great Britain.

"Well, let her out," Sladen ordered. "Get her some food and water."

As word spread throughout the submarine, the fifty-five-man crew had mixed feelings. Some didn't think it was appropriate. Some wanted to kill and eat it. But most thought it was pretty neat to have a reindeer onboard. They even suggested names for their new mascot: Rupert, Randolph, Roland. But those named were nixed because the animal was female.

After some thought, Sladen picked out her name. "She came from Polyarny, so let's call her Pollyanna." It was a play on the name of the port as well as the title of the beloved children's book *Pollyanna*. That story, which he had read to his kids, was about a young orphan who brightens the lives of those around her by always finding a reason to feel glad, no matter how awful the situation.

"Aye, aye, Captain!" said Williams. "Pollyanna, it is."

And so Pollyanna, who slept on a blanket on the floor in the cramped captain's quarters, became the first and only reindeer to live in a submarine. Over the next few days, those crewmen who didn't want the animal aboard soon changed their minds because she was sweet. The adopted calf—a baby reindeer is called a calf, not a fawn—was allowed to stroll through the sub and always brought a smile to the men. There was one thing they didn't like about her—she wasn't potty-trained. The sailors drew cards to see who had to clean up behind her. The smelly job fell to the man with the lowest card.

Every evening when the klaxon made its *ko-hoo-ga* sound to signal that the submarine was surfacing, Pollyanna rushed from her cabin. She stood under the hatch, waiting for someone to open it so she could catch a breath of fresh air. She hogged the spot, often nudging crewmen away. The only person she let near the hatch was the captain, with whom she had formed a bond.

After one week at sea, the *Trident* received new orders: The sub was to patrol the Norwegian Sea between Iceland and Norway for an additional thirty days. The crew groaned when they heard the news. Trotting out the reindeer, Sladen told his mate, "Just like her namesake, let's find the plus side to every bad situation. For us, that means more opportunities to sink an enemy ship."

No one knew how Pollyanna would react in a sea battle. The crew realized she couldn't be ambling around the sub when all hands were busy, so Sladen ordered her locked in his cabin during combat.

After the second week at sea, Pollyanna had eaten all the food that came with her, so the crew fed her scraps from the mess hall, which she enjoyed. She also developed a special liking for evaporated milk.

When the *Trident* arrived in England four weeks later than planned, relatives of the crew were waiting at the dock. Sladen greeted his family with big bear hugs before announcing, "I know it's only November, but I brought you all an early Christmas present that I'm sure you'll never forget."

Just then first mate Williams came over and whispered in Sladen's ear, "Uh, Captain, we have a problem."

"What's the matter?"

The first mate turned his back to Sladen's family and said quietly, "Well, sir, it's Pollyanna. She grew a lot while we were at sea, and now we can't get her out of the hatch."

Sladen stroked his chin and then said, "Okay, here's what to do: Get some of the crew and lay down Pollyanna. While they hold her, tie her legs under her belly. She'll put up a struggle, but it's the only way. Once she's trussed up, they should be able to carry her out."

"Honey, is something wrong?" asked Sladen's wife Sarah.

Sladen faced her and said, "A minor glitch, sweetheart. Now then, what was I talking about?"

"A Christmas present!" shouted Amanda and George in unison.

"Ah yes. I brought you something from the Soviet Union. It should be here soon."

A short while later, Williams, holding a rope looped around the reindeer's neck, gently led the animal down the gangplank and onto the dock.

"Merry Christmas!" cried Sladen to his family.

"Geoffrey, what is it?" asked Sarah.

"A reindeer," Sladen replied. "For you. For all of you."

The kids shrieked with delight and rushed up to the reindeer and petted her.

"Her name is Pollyanna," Sladen said. "And she's ours—a gift from Admiral Petrovich. He said she would be perfect for pulling Elizabeth's pram."

"Oh, darling, I do love the idea, but where will we keep her?" Sarah asked.

"On your parents' farm, of course. She would be free to roam and . . . "

"We can't, sweetheart. While you were away, the Royal Air Force took over the farm to use the land for training. We've moved into a small house in Berwick."

"What will we do, Daddy?" asked Amanda, her lips beginning to tremble. "We can't just turn her loose."

"Well, let's think," said Sladen. "Remember the book *Pollyanna*? She always found the silver lining in everything."

"I have an idea," George said. "Why don't we give her to Father Christmas? Pollyanna won't feel so alone, because she will be with all the other reindeer."

"That's a wonderful suggestion," said Sladen. "But until we can contact Father Christmas, I think Pollyanna will be better off at the London Zoo."

And so the family presented the zoo with a living, breathing Christmas gift.

"I'm sad we couldn't keep her," said Amanda on the way home. "But the zoo people are happy."

"I feel good about it," George added. "It's strange, though. The best Christmas present we ever got is the one we gave away."

For decades, the tale of Pollyanna was considered nothing more than a legend of World War II, because the real facts had long been forgotten. Besides, who would believe that a reindeer lived for weeks aboard a British submarine during wartime? But in 2001, the Royal Navy Submarine Museum in Gosport, Hampshire, England, was given a picture of the late *Trident* skipper Geoffrey Sladen with Pollyanna the reindeer.

The photograph was found when the submariner's family cleaned out old papers and sent them to the museum.

Further checking revealed that a Russian admiral had given Pollyanna as a Christmas gift to Sladen, who then donated her to the zoo. The reindeer adjusted easily to her spacious new surroundings, which were much more comfortable than a submarine. However, she never forgot her time under the sea. Whenever she heard the clanging bell of a fire engine going past the zoo, she would lower her head just as she did when she heard the submarine's klaxon. Pollyanna lived at the zoo until her death in 1946, which occurred only a few days after the *Trident* was decommissioned. ❄

Christmas Miracles

Jesus, Our Brother

Author Unknown, 12th Century

Jesus our brother strong and good,
Was humbly born in a stable rude,
And the friendly beasts around him stood,
Jesus our brother, strong and good

"I," said the donkey, shaggy and brown,
"I carried his mother up hill and down,
I carried her safely to Bethlehem town,
I," said the donkey, shaggy and brown.

"I," said the cow, all white and red,
"I gave him my manger for a bed;
I gave him my hay to pillow his head.
I," said the cow, all white and red.

"I," said the sheep with curly horn,
"I gave him my wool for his blanket warm,
He wore my coat on Christmas morn.
I," said the sheep with curly horn.

"I," said the dove from the rafters high,
"Cooed him to sleep that he should not cry;
We cooed him to sleep, my mate and I.
I," said the dove from the rafters high.

Thus every beast by some good spell,
In the stable dark was glad to tell,
Of the gift he gave Emmanuel,
The gift he gave Emmanuel.

Out of the Night

JACK HARING

Christmas Day 1944
Dear Mom,

This is a very different Christmas Day than I have ever spent in my life. Right now I'm living in the hayloft of a farmer's barn, and I'm very glad to be here rather than out in a foxhole somewhere . . .

The Battle of the Bulge. The final desperate attempt of the Germans to break through Allied lines in Belgium and dash to Antwerp and the sea. For six days, our Eighty-fourth Infantry Division had been diverted from the Ninth Army in the north to the beleaguered First Army area in the Ardennes forest. The fiercest fighting of the war, and I, a nineteen-year-old private, was in the middle of it.

My letter home to Pennsylvania was written on a Christmas morning that was sunny and quiet—deceptively quiet. "The barn I slept in last night," I wrote, "made me think of the place where Jesus came into the world." Then I began reminiscing to Mom about the good Christmases we'd had as I was growing up—always starting with the traditional dawn service at St. John's Lutheran in Boyertown. Church had always been an important part of my life. I'd started college thinking I might go into the ministry.

The letter home was upbeat all the way. I didn't mention anything about the things that had been troubling me. How I had become disillusioned with organized religion because I saw so few Christians either at home or in the combat zone—certainly not Christians trying to live the way Jesus had taught. Or how the weather had been so miserable and the fighting so blazing that I feared I'd never live to see Pennsylvania again.

The last straw was being sent to these snow-covered hills and woods where we might be attacked at any moment from out there, somewhere. I was beginning to think that God had forsaken me.

Still, even though we'd spent the last five days floundering around trying to stop the Germans, even though our supply trucks had been captured, at least we'd had a barn for shelter on Christmas Eve, and our cooks were promising us a hot meal for Christmas Day.

"Let's go, men," Sergeant Presto, our squad leader, shouted. "Collect your gear and fall out. We're going on a mission."

I groaned. We all groaned. There went our first hot meal in a week!

We drove for about ten miles and then the trucks dropped us and sped away. It was dusk. Troops were strung out all along a dirt road that circled through some hills. When Presto came back from a meeting with the platoon leader, he gathered the ten of us—we were one man short in the squad—around him.

"Okay, men, here's what we're going to do. This won't take long and we're going to travel light. Leave your packs and entrenching tools here." He made it sound so simple. Intelligence had said that some German infantry were dug into a nearby hill and were causing havoc by shooting down on the roads in the area. Our battalion's job was to go up and flush them out.

Single file on each side of the winding road, we moved up the hill. We moved quietly, warily. At the top, we were surprised to find, not Germans, but an abandoned chateau in the middle of a clearing. Our squad went into the building. We found a billiard table and the tension broke as we played an imaginary game of pool using our rifles as cues.

Then Presto came stalking in. The Germans, he said, were in the woods beyond the clearing. Our orders were to chase them out into the waiting arms of another battalion positioned at the other end of the woods.

"There'll be three companies in this deal," Presto said. "Two of us will stretch out along the edge of the forest while the other hangs back in reserve. Now, as soon as we push into the woods, everybody fires, got it?"

We spread out and walked through the darkness to the forest's edge; then, at a signal, we burst in, opening up with everything we had. We kept up a brisk pace, keeping contact with our buddies along the moving line, walking and firing for about a mile. But the forest was empty. There was no movement. . . .

The trees in front of us exploded. Suddenly, the night went bright with every kind of firing I'd ever seen or heard of—rifles, rifle-launched grenades, mortars, machine guns, tracers over our heads, bullets at our thighs. But worst of all, Tiger tanks. At least six of them, opening up point-blank with 88-millimeter cannons. Their projectiles whined and crashed all up and down our line.

Our intelligence was wrong, I thought angrily, as I flung myself down on my stomach. *They told us there were no tanks up here. Now we're really in for it.*

Within seconds men were screaming in pain all around me. I saw a tree with a big trunk and made a sudden lunge to get behind it, but I wasn't quick enough. Something tore into my thigh. There was hot, searing pain.

We were completely pinned down. The Tiger tanks kept scanning their turrets and firing on every yard of our line. The German ground troops sent their small-arms fire into anything that moved.

The minutes went by. Five. Ten. Fifteen. Then came a lull in the barrage. I called over to my best buddy, Kane. We called him "Killer." He was the gentlest guy in our platoon, but we'd nicknamed him that after the popular comic strip character "Killer Kane."

"Are you hurt, Killer?"

"Naw. But I think everybody else over here is. Presto's hit bad."

I called to Cruz on my right. He was our squad's B.A.R.man. There was no answer. Then I barely heard him whispering, "I'm hurt. Real bad. Floyd's dead. Corporal John's hit bad."

Well, I thought, *if Presto's out and the Corporal, too, we don't have a leader.*

The pounding started again, this time with flares so they could spot us better. We did some firing back and then the action subsided into another lull.

Down along the rear of our line came a figure, crawling. It was our platoon runner. "Captain says we're getting nowhere," he whispered to Killer and me. "We're pulling back in five minutes. Move out when you hear our covering fire."

I crawled over to Killer. "We've got to get our guys out of here," I said. "You go up your side and I'll go down mine, and we'll drag as many as possible to that big tree back there."

"How're we going to get them out of here, though?"

"I don't know." I said. "But we can't leave them lying here."

We were trapped. I lay there on the cold ground feeling helpless, that forsaken feeling again. Where was the God that I had prayed to during all those years of church and Sunday school back home in Pennsylvania? "And whatsoever ye shall ask in my name, that will I do," the Bible had said to me clearly. Was it necessary, when I needed help so badly, to ask?

"Oh, Lord," I mumbled, "help us. We're trying to get our wounded buddies out of here. Show us the way."

I had no sooner started dragging Corporal John toward our meeting tree when the firing started up in the center of our line. *There's the signal for pulling back,* I thought frantically, *but we can't do it. The Germans will sweep in on us; they'll mop us up before we can pull back.*

Just as I got to the tree, I saw that Killer had brought back three wounded squad members. So we had six in all to get back. I closed my eyes and in desperation said: "In Your name, Lord, help us."

I opened my eyes. In the black of night, moving mysteriously among the shattered trees, a giant hulk came toward us. *The Germans!* My heart thumped. *They've broken out of the brush. They're bearing down on us.* No, it was something else, something unbelievable. It now came into full view and stopped beside our tree.

A horse.

A big, docile, shaggy chestnut, standing there without a harness, as though awaiting our bidding.

Killer and I looked at each other in disbelief. We didn't question then where the horse came from, or how, or why; we just got to work. Moving swiftly, we draped Cruz and the Corporal on the chestnut's broad back, and then Mike and Presto. Then, with Killer carrying one of our buddies and me carrying the other, we led the horse out of the woods. At the

clearing, the horse trotted on ahead of us, straight to the
chateau, and by the time Killer and I got there, our wounded
were already on medical stretchers. The two men we carried in
were cared for; the medics gave a quick look at my shrapnel
wound; and then, as fast as we could, Killer and I went to find
the horse. We wanted to pat him, give him some sugar,
anything to make him sense our gratitude.

But he wasn't there. We looked everywhere, asked everyone
we saw, but no one could tell us anything about him. He had
simply vanished—gone from us as mysteriously as he had
come.

The next morning at the aid station the shrapnel was
removed from my leg, and at noon Killer and I lined up for our
belated Christmas dinner. The day before, 190 men in our
company would have answered the chow call; today there were
thirty-five of us. All the wounded men in our squad had
survived, however, though some were never to see action
again.

Killer and I looked at the turkey and sweet potatoes in our
mess kits. Hot and savory and long-awaited as this food was,
we had no appetite. We were still too full of our emotions: the
sorrow for lost buddies; the shock of our own survival; the

strange, deeply affecting arrival and departure of the horse. We could not get the horse out of our minds then, nor have I since, for that noble creature did more than just save our lives; he reaffirmed my faith. I have always believed that on that Christmas night, God sent that horse to reassure a doubting soldier of his presence, even as he had sent his Son for that purpose on a Christmas night twenty centuries ago. ❄

A Christmas Miracle

*E*very year, we hear that Christmas is becoming *more and more commercial and that the true spirit of the holiday season has been buried under a mountain of material goods. Those at a certain New Hampshire animal shelter can tell a different story. They know the spirit of Christmas is alive and well, and often found in the most unlikely places.*

It was just before Christmas 1999. An angry middle-aged man stood at the counter, gripping the leash of an aging German shepherd. "Why won't you take him?" he shouted. "I need to get him off my hands!"

The adoption counselor tried once more to explain. "At fourteen, Samson is too old to be a good adoption candidate," she said. "Plus, he has already developed some age-related illnesses and infirmities. I know he is a wonderful dog, but it is really unlikely that someone would adopt him."

"Well, then, just take him and put him down!" the man yelled. "I want to get rid of him."

"We don't take animals just to put them down," the counselor explained. "May I ask, after all this time, why you no longer wish to keep the dog?"

"I just can't stand the sight of him," the man hissed, "and if you won't put him down, I'll shoot him myself."

Trying not to show her horror, the counselor pointed out that shooting an animal was illegal. She urged the man to consult with his veterinarian for other options.

"I'm not spending any more money on this animal," the man grumbled and, yanking the leash, he stalked out.

Concerned, the counselor wrote down the license plate of the man's truck and offered up a quick prayer for Samson.

A few days later, a German shepherd was found abandoned. He was brought to the shelter, and the staff recognized him as Samson. The town where he was abandoned was where his owner lived. The man was contacted by police and, under questioning, admitted he had tried to get rid of the dog. Distraught over a recent divorce, the man sought revenge through the shepherd. He hadn't even wanted the dog, but he fought to keep him to spite his wife. Once his wife was gone, he couldn't bear to see the animal. The man was charged with abandonment, and Samson came to stay at the shelter. The wife and the couple's son were located in Pennsylvania. They were horrified to hear what had happened to their dog, and agreed immediately to have him come live with them. There was just one problem. . . .

The wife was nearly broke after the divorce and their initial move. She could take no time off from work to drive to New Hampshire and get the dog, and she couldn't afford any other method of bringing him to her. She hated to have Samson in the shelter any longer but didn't know what to do. "We'll come up with something," the staff assured her, but in their hearts they didn't know what. They were concerned as well. Samson had lived in a family home all his life. Within a few weeks, his whole world had been turned upside down. He was beginning to pine, and staffers could tell by his eyes that if he wasn't back with his family soon, he would give up.

Christmas was only two weeks away when the angel arrived. He arrived by pickup truck and in the form of a man in his mid-thirties. Through a friend of a shelter staffer, he had heard about Samson's plight. He was willing to drive Samson to Pennsylvania, and he would do it before Christmas.

The staff was thrilled with the offer, but cautious. Why would a perfect stranger drive hundreds of miles out of his way to deliver a dog to people he didn't know? They had to make sure he was legitimate and that Samson wouldn't be sold to meat dealers or other unscrupulous purchasers or dumped along the interstate.

The man understood their concerns and, thankfully, checked out to be an upstanding citizen. In the course of the conversation, he admitted why he had come forward.

"Last year, I left my dog in my van while I went inside to do some grocery shopping," he explained. "While I was inside, something made the van catch fire. I heard people hollering, and I rushed out to see my van engulfed in flames. I thought I would die. My dog means everything to me, and he was trapped. I tried to get to the van, but people restrained me. Then, I heard someone shouting, 'The dog is safe! The dog is safe!' I looked over, and there was this man I'd never seen before holding my dog. He had risked his own life to get my dog out. I'll forever be in his debt. Just when you don't think there are heroes anymore, one comes along.

"I vowed then and there that if I ever had the chance to do someone a good turn when it came to a beloved pet, I would. When I heard about Samson and his family, I knew this was my chance, so here I am."

The shelter staff was amazed. They all knew about the van rescue story. It had been in all the papers, and the shelter had even given the rescuer a reward, but they had never dreamed that Samson's angel was connected to this earlier good deed.

A few days later, Samson and his angel were on their way. The dog seemed to know he was going home, because his ears perked up and his eyes were brighter than they had been in some time.

Just before Christmas, the mail brought one of the best cards the shelter had ever received. Along with a thank-you note were photos of a deliriously happy Samson romping with his family in the snow, and snuggled with them by their Christmas tree. Samson was truly where he belonged, and the staff knew he would live out his days happily there.

They also knew that Samson's journey home was a true Christmas miracle—and that angels—and heroes—may still appear when you need them, even in the most unlikely forms. ❄

Catfish Promises

ANNE CULBREATH WATKINS

*C*hristmas 1998 looked very bleak for my husband Allen and me. Allen was a full-time touring musician and his work had slowed down for the winter. Without a steady paycheck, we fell behind on our bills, and things added up in a hurry. We knew we'd be all right once the touring season started back, but the mortgage and the other bills couldn't wait that long. Foreclosure loomed over our heads, and I worried myself sick about our finances.

And then, just two days before Christmas, a crippling ice storm struck. Beautiful, deadly, unforgiving ice covered the power lines and tree limbs all through the county. Our rural area was especially hard hit—hundreds of trees snapped under the weight of the ice. They sounded like gunshots going off in the woods behind our house. Later that night I heard the heating unit shut off and knew our electricity had been lost. I shook Allen awake. "Help me cover the fish tanks!" I cried. It wouldn't take long for the fish to die once they started getting cold. And the funny little scavengers, our corydora catfish, had just laid eggs all over the tank walls a few days ago. This would surely kill them.

We tossed blankets and quilts over the three tanks. The water was still warm, but the temperature in the house would begin falling soon. Our two parrots were snug in their cages, blankets keeping drafts away from their small bodies. I knew they'd be all right as long as we kept them covered. But the aquariums . . . my heart sank when I thought about losing all our lovely fish.

There was an old kerosene heater stored on the porch and Allen lugged it inside. Fortunately we had a container of kerosene stored with it and soon had a warm blaze going. We closed off rooms that didn't need the heat and made sure the door was open to the room in the back of the house where our largest aquarium stood. Tired and worried, we went back to bed. I prayed that we wouldn't get up the next morning to find a lot of dead fish.

To our surprise, the house was warm when we got up. Too warm, in fact! The kerosene heater's thermostat switch didn't work and there was no way to adjust the heat. It must have been eighty degrees in the house.

We quickly checked the thermometers in all the aquariums. The temperatures were holding steady, pretty close to what they'd been when the power went off. And all the fish were doing fine, swimming around in their darkened tanks, acting no different from usual.

Over the next few days we discovered that lots of foods could be prepared over a kerosene heater—beans, eggs and sausages, soup, coffee, even biscuits. At night, when there was no television to watch or stereo to listen to, we got out Allen's guitar and sang our favorite songs. Sometimes we squinted in the semidarkness over the Scrabble board, or sat closer to the lamps and strained our eyes trying to read. The house was toasty warm and the birds seemed to be enjoying the adventure. Still, my heart sank lower with each passing moment. What were we going to do about all those bills? Somehow, sitting in the near darkness made everything seem worse.

Christmas day arrived, cold, icy and still with no electricity. We trudged next door to my brother's house, where he had rigged up an electric light bulb to a car battery. We had a wonderful time, opening gifts in the soft light and enjoying a fantastic hot meal cooked on their gas stove. Then Allen and I walked back home, slipping and sliding on the ice-covered road, breathing in great gasps of frigid air. Brilliant stars glowed in the darkness overhead and I tried to imagine how the night skies must have looked to the shepherds all those years ago. Was it as cold and blustery then as it was now?

It was a relief to hustle into our warm house, and I hurriedly checked the aquariums with a flashlight. Everybody was still swimming around, and the temperature in the tanks was a few degrees higher than normal. That old kerosene heater was doing its job well. As I dropped food into the tanks, I caught myself breathing a prayer. "Dear God, if we have dead fish when the electricity comes back on, I'll know we're going to lose the house. If all the fish are okay, we'll be okay too." I knew it was silly, but I found myself clinging to those words over the next few days.

New Year's Eve was rapidly approaching and the power was still off. Some of the roads were passable now and we went out to survey the damage. Our area looked like a war zone. Trees were snapped off, power poles broken, homes damaged, cars crushed under fallen trees. The devastation was widespread and nobody seemed to have any idea when our electricity would be restored.

I checked on the fish often. It was hard to count them in the dark, but I was afraid to take the blankets off the tanks. I'd rather strain my eyes trying to see than to risk chilling them. From what I could tell, we hadn't lost anybody yet. So far, so good.

Then came the day we'd been praying for. There was a hum, a few odd crackling noises, and the lights snapped on. Life was soon back to normal. Allen even got a call to work with a friend of his who needed some carpentry work done, and while this would certainly help our finances, I was afraid it would be too little, too late. With a heavy heart, I went to watch the fish.

There was movement in the big busy plant in the corner of one of the tanks. "What is that?" I muttered. I stooped down so I could peer more closely into the tank. A teensy baby catfish was busily cleaning the plant leaves!

The prayer I'd caught myself whispering over and over since Christmas night exploded in my mind. "If the fish die, we'll lose the house. If the fish are okay, we'll be okay too."

Suddenly, my heart sang with joy. Not only had all the fish survived, but we had brand-new baby catfish! I knew that everything was going to be all right, thanks to Christmas prayers and promises—and a few little catfish. ❄

Saved by Dolphins

ANNE ARCHER

*I*t was Christmas vacation, and I went home for the holiday to visit my mother on Hilton Head Island, South Carolina. I loved coming to the island. It renewed my sense of self and restored my health. Here I felt connected to my roots, nature and the vast oceans. At the time of this visit, on Christmas Day, I had graduated from college and was teaching high school. I loved my work, but it was very demanding physically, emotionally and mentally. The island was a sanctuary where I felt that the universe might actually hear my call for renewal.

I longed to just dive into the ocean and swim until I could swim no more. I wanted to vent my energies and relax totally. Always a strong swimmer, I was called a fish by my family because I taught myself to swim at age two. As a child, I'd swim long distances, staying in the water all day and loving every moment.

Around noon on this holiday, I went to the beach and walked alone on the warm sands along the water's edge. The sun was brilliant, but most people sitting on the beach probably thought that the winter was too cool for swimming.

Vacationers on this international beach resort greeted me with a variety of accents as I gathered shells.

When I felt warm enough, I walked into the ocean waves and dove in. I swam hard and fast. Even when I felt tired, I continued. At last I rolled over on my back and looked toward the beach. I was amazed to be so far away from the shore. The people on the beach were tiny specks and a large expanse of ocean waves separated us.

This had been my family home for years, so I knew these waters well. My mind raced to warnings I'd received. The few sharks that had ever been seen in the area were known to be attracted to shrimp boats, but none were in sight. Even though no one else was in the water, I didn't feel frightened.

I began my long swim back with strong strokes. I loved the smell of the fresh salt air. The water's temperature had become comfortable. I swam in total abandon until I again checked the shoreline. It was as if I'd barely moved. I could feel myself being pulled out to sea. Trying not to panic, I reminded myself that people watching me from the shore had probably seen how far I'd gone out.

Suddenly I was frozen with fear, because off to my left a dark fin moved directly toward me. My heart pounded wildly.

I stopped swimming and attempted to float and bob in the water, stretched out like a log on the surface. I could barely breathe. I closed my eyes. I tried desperately to keep my mind from entertaining the horrors of being eaten by a shark. Suddenly a powerful, smooth, sleek body rose underneath me.

I couldn't imagine what was happening. I felt my body being lifted slightly. While gliding across the water's surface, I was being moved toward the shore. Then slowly, gently, I was lowered back into the ocean. I instantly felt the strange sensation of a powerful body rising up and then lifting and carrying me forward.

The surface of the water broke in front of me and I could finally see the creature that was carrying me. It was a beautiful dolphin who jumped through the air, looked at me, dived to the left, and dipped underwater again. All the while, I moved through the water at great speed while another of those wonderful animals appeared. Soon I was surrounded by a school of dolphins. One at a time they moved beneath me, lifting and carrying me back to shore as if they were performing an orchestrated dance or choreographed ballet.

The dolphins took turns carrying me and then leaping in front and moving around. One to the left. One to the right.

Quickly and smoothly, they brought me to chest-high water. Then they encircled me, spinning, diving, smiling. The dolphins called in an amazing, high-pitched language that filled me with delight. I clapped in appreciation for the show they were providing. Touched and in awe, I couldn't stop talking to and thanking them. Eventually they turned, said farewell, and danced out to sea. ❄

Sometimes Angels Come in Disguise

RENIE SZILAK BURGHARDT

*I*t was a cold but sunny December afternoon as I headed up the old lane leading to the cedar woods. It would be a half-mile walk, and I carried a bow saw and a transistor radio playing Christmas music. Apropos for ten days before Christmas.

Ever since I moved from the city to these beautiful, wild Ozark hills, it had become a ritual, this walk to the cedar woods to cut down my Christmas tree. A pleasant ritual it was too—the climb of a steep hill, the vast stretches of hardwood forest, and finally, the green oasis of the cedar woods. I loved it all.

When I reached the cedar woods, I startled a large, noisy flock of robins that had obviously opted to spend the winter among the cedars instead of migrating to warmer surroundings. And why not? The cedars provided plenty of cedar berries to feed on and shelter from the cold winds among their dense, green boughs. A perfect refuge for bird or beast, I thought.

I walked on among the cedars, admiring the cylindrical shapes, some twenty feet tall, some just a few inches above ground. Each time I saw one that seemed perfect for my purpose, I would see another one, even more perfect, up ahead. Finally, I chose one about three feet tall, and got down on my knees to cut it with my bow saw. I would decorate it later that evening.

Task done, with the little cedar in one gloved hand, the bow saw in the other, I headed for the lane. Just in time, too, I thought to myself, for it was getting chilly. However, it soon dawned on me that the lane seemed nowhere in sight. I glanced at my watch nervously. It was already three o'clock in the afternoon. Had I been in these woods two hours? Then, as another hour passed with still no sign of the familiar lane, I began to panic.

How could I have gotten myself lost? I had been in these woods many times, since hiking is one of my favorite pastimes, and I was pretty sure I knew my way around. Suddenly, my daughter's call from the city the night before came to mind. "A sixty-year-old woman should not be traipsing around in the woods by herself," she had said. And I had laughed at her. Now, the prospect of spending the night in the woods on a freezing December night didn't seem one bit funny. Tears welled in my eyes as I continued walking.

After a while, I glanced at my watch again. It was four o'clock. The sun was going down and I was getting more scared by the minute. Finally I sat on a fallen log and decided a prayer could not hurt my predicament. I had always turned to God in the past. He had never let me down.

As I sat there, head bowed, eyes closed, I suddenly felt a pair of eyes watching me. I opened my eyes and saw her.

It was a doe, standing less than twenty feet away, gazing at me unafraid. She was beautiful.

"I know you never become lost. You know your way around the woods. But I'm not like you. I'm only a human. And I'm definitely lost," I called out to her.

"Follow me."

I didn't exactly hear the words. It was like a thought transfer, instead. And it was coming from the deer! I stood up, grabbed my tree and bow saw, and began to follow her through the woods. I decided that even if this was a hallucination, I had nothing to lose since I was already lost.

Less than ten minutes later, I was back on familiar ground.

"Thank you, angel deer," I called out to the doe. She looked back at me and then bounded off into the woods, her white tail waving good-bye.

Then it was my turn to bound off toward the house. I reached it just as darkness descended. "Thank You, Lord," I whispered toward the heavens as I opened my front door. Inside, my phone was ringing.

"Where have you been? I called twice already!" my worried daughter asked.

"I was lost in the woods," I told her. "But an angel in disguise showed me the way back." Then I told her what had happened.

"I'm taking your granddaughters to see Santa tomorrow. I think we will put in a special request for you this year," she finally said.

On Christmas morning, there was a small gift marked "From Santa" under my Christmas tree. It turned out to be a compass. I never go to the woods without it these days. ❄

Christmas Morning in the Pasture

BETTY ELROD

*T*emperatures dropped, but no matter. Our house was warm as toast. I put finishing touches on the holiday decorations. Jackson, our Yorkshire terrier, watched me hang my stocking and then Bill's. He cocked his head.

"Do you think I'd forget you on Christmas Eve?" I pulled out the plaid stocking with Jackson embroidered at the top and hung it next to ours. Jackson wagged his tail. He might not have been able to read his name, but after fifteen years he knew his stocking.

I snaked some garland into the hallway. A pile of Christmas cards lay on the side table by the door. Several of them were addressed to Jackson. "To one of my favorite customers," wrote Jan from the grooming salon. "Merry Christmas!" He also got cards from all of our grandchildren.

Anybody who found it silly for a dog to get this much attention didn't know Jackson. That dog had personality. When I took him for walks, neighbors bent down to talk to him. "You look very handsome in your yellow slicker," a friend told Jackson one rainy day. Jackson ran around in a circle, showing off. Even four-legged neighbors weren't immune to his charms. Our backyard bordered a pasture where horses grazed. They came right up to the wire fence and put their massive heads down low. Jackson wasn't intimidated. He ran over to say hello, barking, jumping, begging to be noticed.

I arranged Jackson's Christmas cards so Bill would see them when he got home from work. Taking care of our little dog was a big focus. But we couldn't protect Jackson from everything. He was getting older. His eyesight was almost gone. He could barely hear. Sometimes he got confused outside and couldn't find his way back to the house. What if something happened when Bill and I weren't home? Who would protect him then?

Jackson barked and hurried into the living room. "You always know the time. Don't you, boy?" I laughed. Right on schedule Jackson climbed up on the couch and watched for Bill. "Somebody got a lot of cards," I sang when he came in, "and it wasn't you or me." Bill chuckled at each one.

We had a quiet evening, just the three of us. After dinner, Bill and Jackson played fetch with a crocheted jingle ball. We turned in early. "Santa won't come till you're fast asleep," I teased Jackson. Bill and I slipped underneath the covers. Jackson curled up at our feet with his stuffed lamb. "Night, Jackson," I said before I drifted off.

I awoke some time later, hearing a bark in the darkness. "Jackson has to go out," I mumbled. I rolled over to look at the clock: 3:00 AM. "Be right back," Bill said. I must have dozed off. This time Bill was shaking me. "What is it?"

"Jackson's gone!"

My eyes darted to Jackson's usual spot on the bed. Only his stuffed lamb was there.

Bill was shivering in his pajamas. "I thought he'd stick close to the porch. I just ran in for my robe."

I pulled on some sweatpants. Bill grabbed a flashlight. We headed for the back door. "Jackson!" I called from the porch. "Jackson!" No answer. An icy wind whipped through my hair. "It's freezing. That old dog won't last out here."

"Let's ride around," Bill suggested. We went to the car. Bill drove and I searched out the windows. Jackson was nowhere to be found. Bill and I returned home. "Jackson!" we yelled in the yard. I panned a flashlight beam across the bushes. "Here, boy!"

What was that? A faint bark in the distance. Bill and I looked past the fence. "It came from the pasture!" I cried.

Bill helped me over the fence that separated our yard from the field. I hadn't climbed a fence in I don't know how long, but I would have climbed Mount Everest for Jackson. Bill was right behind me. Searching wasn't easy in the dark. The barking—if that's what it was—had stopped. Which way to go? My fingers and toes ached from the cold. "We'll come back in the morning," Bill said finally, sweeping the grass with the flashlight one more time.

Heartbroken, we trudged back to the house. Jackson was cold and alone. No one to protect him. Not even his stuffed lamb for comfort. I wrapped my coat around my shoulders. *Lord, keep Jackson safe and warm*. It seemed like an impossible prayer on a night like this. But anything was possible on Christmas, wasn't it?

It was close to 5:00 AM. Bill and I sat at the kitchen table, waiting for first light. We never said what we both were thinking: We probably wouldn't find Jackson alive. After what seemed like forever, the first rays of dawn appeared through the window. "Merry Christmas," said Bill. "Let's go find our boy."

We headed back to the pasture, empty save for four majestic horses. I'd never noticed how beautiful they were until now. The soft light caught their smooth coats and settled around them like a fleece blanket. "Look, Bill. They know how to protect themselves from this cold." Heads bent toward the ground, the horses stood together in a huddle, warmed by the breaths of one another. It was an almost heavenly scene. Peaceful as it was, though, it only brought tears to my eyes. If those big, strong animals felt the cold, there was no way Jackson could have survived it. My throat was sore from calling.

"Maybe we should take the car out again," Bill said.

I called once more. "Jackson!" A high-pitched whine answered. I looked at Bill—he'd heard it too. It came from over where the horses stood. We rushed to them. I squeezed my body into the center of their circle.

"What's going on here?" I asked the gentle creatures. Something was there on the ground between their feet. A furry animal, curled up tight. I swept aside the tall grass with my hand. A tiny tongue licked my finger. Jackson!

One of the horses tossed its head and snorted proudly. "We took care of him. We kept him safe," the great beast seemed to say. The other horses crowded their large bodies close, blocking Jackson from the wind and warming him with their breath. I gathered our little dog up in my arms and wrapped him in my scarf, rocking him like a baby. Jackson whimpered and licked my nose. "You scared us there, Jackson," Bill said, ruffling his ears.

The horses slowly backed away. They swished their tails and munched the grass, hungry after their night's work. We had quite a story to tell the kids and grandkids over Christmas dinner. Jackson's angels had manes instead of wings!

I didn't worry so much about Jackson after that. I knew in my heart he was watched over. When he died, Bill and I were by his side. I believe angels huddled around us, too, comforting our baby like the horses had that peaceful Christmas morning. But this time Jackson's angels had wings. ❄

Christmas

ERIC SWANSON

*T*hose were hard years," Ida Mackenzie recalls. "Even as children, we could see the worry on Mom and Dad's faces, on the faces of our neighbors who ran the farm across the way, on the people we'd see on the street when we went into town. We had food on the table and a roof over our heads, but we'd hear our parents talking at night—their voices came up through the floor or through the walls—and we understood it was a miracle sometimes that they found a way to make ends meet. They say there's no good times for kids to grow up really, but those were hard times."

She's speaking, of course, about the Great Depression that followed the stock market crash of 1929. By 1932, hundreds of banks had failed, and scores of mills, factories and other businesses had shut their doors for good. More than ten million people lost their jobs, and with no livelihood to support workers or consumers, farms and homes across the nation were foreclosed. In spite of emergency farm relief and public works projects, the Great Depression grew steadily worse.

Mackenzie, a Minnesota native, vividly remembers her parents' struggle to keep the modest family farm running. They had to sell off livestock and let go of workers whose families they'd known for two or three generations. Dwindling resources made it absolutely necessary to conserve fuel during the harsh northwestern winters, when temperatures sometimes dipped twenty or thirty degrees below freezing. At the time, the blessings of a large family outweighed the difficulties.

"My three sisters and I huddled together in one bed to keep warm, and my three brothers did the same in another," Mackenzie explains. "We all pitched in with the chores just to keep the farm running. Things weren't so bad in the summer, but in the winter—how I hated getting out of bed at four in the morning and making my way down to the cold kitchen and then out to the barn."

One frosty morning shortly after Thanksgiving, twelve-year-old Ida and her eight-year-old brother Clint made a remarkable discovery. As they entered the barn to milk the two remaining family cows, a gray tabby cat poked his head out from one of the empty stalls. "Clint wanted to chase the cat away," Ida recalls. "He didn't have much use for cats. He thought they were more sneaky than anything else. 'Course, he changed his tune pretty quickly once we found out what that cat had dragged in with him, so to speak."

As Ida's brother ran toward the cat, the animal retreated into the stall, but only so far as a small mound of hay piled up along the wall. There the cat not only stood his ground but to both children's amazement actually emitted a low hiss—or as Ida describes it, "a pathetic little noise, like the last bit of air from a bicycle tire." Ida motioned her brother to stay behind, and she stepped slowly toward the tabby, holding out her hand and making soft, clicking sounds with her tongue. The cat held its ground but allowed her to approach. About a foot from the mound of hay now, Ida at last made out what the cat had been protecting.

"Holy geez," she remembers crying to her brother. "Clint, there's a baby here!"

The infant boy was dressed in pants, shirt, socks and a little wool hat and wrapped in a blanket made, as Ida recalls, of "a thin sort of burlap." As she lifted the infant to examine it for signs of life, Ida couldn't help but notice that the blanket was covered with cat hair. Evidently, the cat had slept on top of the boy, warming him like an incubator and virtually guaranteeing his safety through the cold winter night. Nor was he willing to give up his charge once it had been delivered safely into human hands. As Ida carried the child across the field back to the house, the cat followed at her heels.

At first, Ida's mother refused to allow the animal into the house. But after the children recounted the story of his protective behavior, she relented. "Or rather," Ida is quick to clarify, "she didn't so much give in as stop refusing to let us let him in. She didn't think much of the idea of a cat in the house, but she recognized a good deed when she saw one." The cat seemed to grasp the rules immediately. Rather than jump up on the table where Ida's mother had laid the child for a closer examination, he simply stood at polite attention a few feet away to watch the proceedings.

Despite the hardship of raising an extra child, Ida's parents were determined to foster the infant, at least for a while. Ida suspects her parents knew whose child he was and believed that one day—perhaps when times improved—his real parents would come forward to claim him. Ultimately, they adopted the boy, formally giving him the name Joe, as in Joseph from the Christmas story. "Because he came to us so close to Christmas," Ida explains. "We called the cat Christmas for the same reason, as a matter of fact. Though maybe we should have named him Santa Claus. But that would have been too confusing for my little brothers and sisters, I think."

According to Ida, Joe grew up strong and healthy—a hard worker, always willing to pitch in. "I'm sure he was grateful to my parents for taking him in," she adds, "even though it's still not the happiest of endings. We lost him in Korea, when he was just shy of twenty years old."

And what of Christmas?

"He was a barn cat," Ida replies. "He never liked being in the house much. It probably cramped his style. Once he knew Joe was all right, he preferred going back to the barn. He made a nice place for himself there and kept the mice away during the summer. And of course, every Christmas he got a bowl of milk or a helping of turkey—a special little present all his own." ❄

The Blessing of the Animals

God's Love

SAMUEL TAYLOR COLERIDGE

He prayeth well who loveth well,
　　Both man and bird and beast;
He prayeth best who loveth best,
　　All things both great and small;
For the dear God who loveth us,
　　He made and loveth all.

A Moment in the Barn

Nancy McGuirk

I was determined to make Christmas perfect.
Our home, an old stucco farmhouse, looked like
something out of a magazine. From the red-ribboned
wreath on the front door to the row of hand-knit stockings
hanging from the mantel and my best china laid out on the
table, ready for a feast. I took a deep breath. *Please, Lord, let this
Christmas be everything it's supposed to be,* I begged. But could it,
now that my husband and I had separated? Would Christmas
ever be the same for me and my kids?

The kids were upstairs, working on last-minute secret
projects and changing for church. I checked the ham in the
oven and then washed my hands in the sink. The muscles in
my neck and shoulders felt tight and achy. I was so tired from
trying to make everything right. Tired from feeling
bitter, frightened, abandoned. I just want to have someone
come and take care of me for a while, I thought.

That reminded me. Out the window I could see across the
yard to the darkened barn. "Greg?" I called up the stairs. No
answer. "Could one of you girls please ask your brother if he's
fed the animals yet?" I asked.

"He's in the shower, Mom," one said. "He hasn't fed them and wants to know if you'd do it for him."

I sighed. Sometimes it was just easier to take care of something myself rather than make a big deal about it. I pulled off my high heels and stuffed myself—still in my church dress and pearls—into heavy-duty zippered coveralls. Then I put on my muddy barn boots, tugged on my warm gloves and a ski cap and stepped outside.

The cool air revived me somewhat. I trudged up the walk and opened the barnyard gate. Our farm wasn't large—only ten acres. But the maintenance was daunting and constant. The children had their chores to take care of both inside and out. It had only been two months since my husband left. The kids and I were still trying to get the hang of running things on our own.

I flicked on the lights inside the barn and saw that everyone was assembled: two Hereford steers, one gray Appaloosa mare, a rust-colored quarter horse and a half-dozen pigeons. They started jockeying for position at the feed troughs. In the feed room I measured two overflowing scoops into two different buckets—one for the horses and one for the steers. The pigeons would have to fend for themselves.

I splashed grain into the two horse feeders and then pushed and clucked to get the horses over to their side of the barn. Once they were headed in the right direction, I spilled grain in a line down the cattle trough. Then I climbed up the ladder to the hay bales. I broke a bale apart and tossed a few slabs onto the hard mud floor below.

Then it was back down to crack the ice in the livestock waterer. I took off my gloves, squatted and reached for the faucet. I turned on the spigot and got the water level back up. I stood up and dusted myself off. The animals were eating contentedly. Everything seemed in order. I just hoped my dress and stockings would be relatively unbesmirched when I got the coveralls off. I flipped off the light switch on the beam and closed the half-door to the feed-room hall. And I stood there till my eyes adjusted to the dark.

In that quiet blackness, all my senses sharpened. I heard the slow crunch-crunch-crunch of the steers and horses munching their grain and the flutter of wings as the pigeons hopped around looking for stray kernels among shifting hooves. The stamping of feet, swishing of tails and low throaty moos made a kind of music in the air. The rich scents of loamy earth and crisp night air and grain and hay flooded my nostrils.

What a wonderful place this barn is, I thought. I hadn't felt so at peace in a long while.

Is that why you chose to be born in a barn, Lord? Away from the hustle and bustle, surrounded only by the simple creatures of earth? Away from the worries and tribulations of this world?

By now, my eyes had adjusted fully to the darkness. And the stillness I felt changed too. It became alive, pulsing with something majestic, something holy. There was a presence in this old barn, as close to me as the mud on my hands and the pearls around my neck. Wonder and awe washed over me, and the pain and anger and rejection in my heart melted. So did everything else I was feeling. Every problem and every worry I had fell away. I felt as if nothing stood between me and God's love for me.

You are so much love, I thought. I leaned against the rough timber of the doorpost for a long time, drawing in that feeling of being cared for, of being absolutely loved. I drew it in as hungrily as the animals devoured their feed. I felt a new strength fill me, one that would not fail or abandon me.

No, perhaps Christmas would never be the same for me or my family. But the glad tidings of that first Christmas in Bethlehem were not expressed in a pretty dinner table laid with fine china, a beautifully decorated house or a candlelight church service, or in anything else I could do. The good news was in the overpowering reality of Christ's birth, and the love that lit our darkness like the brightest star.

On that Christmas Eve he came to a barn once again, just to remind me of that love. ❄

Time for McGee

JEANNE GORE

*W*hy wouldn't this cat leave me alone? I put my hands to his plush blue-gray fur and pushed him gently off my computer keyboard where I was typing up minutes from yet another committee meeting. McGee yawned and tapped me playfully with his paw.

"I have a lot of work to do before bed," I told him. "No time for your games." McGee flicked his tail lazily and gazed up at me with emerald green eyes. He was a beautiful cat and a rare breed, according to our vet: a Russian blue.

"I don't know how you can resist him," said my husband Donald from the doorway. McGee wasn't my cat, he was Donald's. He was the one who insisted we take in the stray. Besides, it wasn't in my nature to turn my back on something that needed doing. Like balancing the accounts for our church council and volunteering for the art center, the food cupboard and a local theater company—on top of my paying job.

I'd always enjoyed taking on projects, helping out in the community, solving problems. The more I accomplished, the more energized I felt. These past few months, though, all the work I'd loved turned into pure drudgery. My arms and legs felt weighted down. I wasn't sleeping well. I couldn't focus. I had to push myself to get going in the morning. Thanksgiving dinner had wiped me out, and now Christmas was just around the corner.

McGee pressed a paw to my keyboard. A line of *m*'s shot across the screen. "No, McGee!" I ordered. "Donald, please do something with this cat."

Donald took McGee from the desk and carried him into another room. But not before McGee gave me a good hard stare. It was as if he was determined to have his way, no matter what.

The next morning I grabbed a quick breakfast, afraid if I sat down with a cup of tea I might not get back up. I headed for the door. Something silky brushed against my leg. "McGee, I'm in a hurry."

McGee twined himself around one ankle and then the other, making a lazy figure eight. I couldn't leave without stepping on him. I bent down and gave his head a rub. "Okay, I've said good-bye to you. Can I go now? Please?" McGee rubbed his head insistently against my hand, tilting his face up at me. "Don't look at me like that. I'll see you after work—for a second, anyway, before I run out to a committee meeting."

I supposed my life did look pretty strange to a cat, all my coming and going. But McGee didn't appreciate the responsibilities I had. Too many to while away the minutes stroking a cat.

After work I ran into the house to grab some papers. "Now, where are my keys?" I muttered, plopping into a chair to hunt through my purse.

McGee leapt up into my lap, almost knocking my purse to the floor. "Well, hello to you too!" I said. McGee kneaded my lap with his paws and then curled into a ball. Donald looked on, amused. "I wanted to get to the meeting early," I said, "but he's got me trapped."

"I've got to hand it to him," Donald said. "It's not easy to get you to sit still."

I rubbed McGee under his chin. He purred. I had to admit, this little respite wasn't such a bad idea. I didn't get to the meeting early, but I was on time. And I felt the slightest jump in my step.

That night I was back at the computer. The words on the screen ran together in a blur. I shut my eyes for a moment, hoping to clear my head. When I opened them, McGee was sitting on the floor beside my chair, his front paws held up in the air like he was begging. "That's a dog trick, McGee. You're a cat!"

As if he understood, McGee chased his tail round and round in a circle. I laughed until tears came to my eyes. McGee tumbled around at my feet. I turned off the computer. Work could wait until the show was over.

"What's going on in here, you two?" Donald wanted to know.

"Have you ever seen McGee's begging trick? Or watched him chase his tail?"

"He does that stuff all the time, Jeanne. I guess you've been missing out."

Well, that was enough of that. A few days later I was making out a shopping list for the afternoon. What I really wanted to do was nap, but I had a lot of presents to pick out before Christmas. *I'll show Donald and McGee. I'll just lie here on the couch for five minutes.*

Those five minutes were up much too soon, but I'd proved that I knew how to take a breather when I needed it. I started to get up. McGee jumped on the couch, right onto my stomach. He settled down with a warm, heavy weight. He laid his head on my chest and stretched out his body as long as it would go until he covered me like a cozy blanket. The heat from his body sank into me. One by one, my muscles relaxed. *I don't want to disturb McGee. Maybe I'll stay put.*

I must have drifted off. "Why didn't you wake me up?" I asked Donald. "I've wasted valuable shopping time."

"You looked so peaceful sleeping there," he said. "Dr. McGee must have thought you needed the rest."

McGee looked at me. He seemed awfully pleased with himself. *Okay, McGee,* I thought. *You win.* I had to admit I'd woken refreshed and ready to meet the rest of my day. More like my old happy-to-be-busy self.

By the time Christmas rolled around I'd forgotten how I'd been dreading it. I juggled wrapping presents with baking cookies and helping out at church. But I no longer felt overburdened and tired. I stopped worrying about "wasting" time—on McGee or a hot cup of tea or an afternoon nap. In fact, I felt like I had more time than ever. Time for myself and the people—and the cat—I loved.

"Here I thought we were watching out for you," I told McGee on Christmas Eve as he followed me to answer the front door. "But I think maybe God sent you to watch over me instead."

It was my neighbor, dropping by with a present. McGee jumped up next to me on the sofa. I unwrapped an illustrated book on cats.

"Let's see what it has to say about Russian blues," I said.

"Look, McGee!" I pointed to the entry. Russian blues were sometimes called Arkhangelsk, after the northern port where Western sailors first saw the heavenly breed. An archangel cat? Those sailors were definitely onto something. Like McGee was onto me. ❅

"For-the-Birds" Christmas

MAY SHERIDAN GOLD

*J*t started off as a miserable Advent. All three children were confined to the house with the flu and I didn't know how to perk up their sad little spirits as Christmas approached. They were getting bored and restless. I had my hands full with shopping, decorating and baking, with very little time left over to entertain them.

One morning I found them crouched in the dining room staring at something outside the floor-length window. I tiptoed behind them to catch a glimpse of what was occupying their attention, when they jumped up and pulled me down to their level.

"Look, Mother," Elizabeth, the youngest, cried. "See the red birds and the sparrows hopping around on the snow? They're probably hungry and don't know where to get food." I watched in fascination as the tiny creatures bobbed up and down, fluttering in the snow and around the majestic evergreen that adorned a corner of our yard.

"Couldn't we do something?" Andy, my ten-year-old, pleaded.

"Yeah," Skip, eight, agreed, "maybe we could put some plates of bread crumbs outside."

"No," said Andy, "the cats will get them. Can't we put them on the evergreen?" Three round faces looked eagerly at me for approval.

"I think that's a wonderful idea, children," I said, proud of their concern for the poor birds. "Let's go in the kitchen and see what we can come up with." The three eager beavers trotted behind me, and for the next hour we were on a scavenger hunt in the kitchen: popcorn, cranberries, sunflower seeds, raisins, apples, even peanut butter—the children were very inventive!

For the next few days and evenings, trimming the tree for the birds became our family project. Hours were spent making the decorations, and each evening my husband Dan or I went outside and hung them on the evergreen tree—some on strings and some attached with pipe cleaners. The children were so busy and excited, they soon forgot their confinement and were back in good health before Christmas arrived.

Now, each Christmas at our house is "for-the-birds," as well as for our family. Maybe you'd like to start this family tradition at your house. Here are some of the items we've used.

- Strings of popcorn
- Strings of cranberries

- Old jar tops: Spread each with a mixture of peanut butter and one tablespoon or more of corn meal; or spread with cold bacon fat. Press into these mixtures sunflower seeds, raisins, cranberries, other bird seed.

- Coffee can tops: Again, spread with peanut butter mixture and with cranberries or raisins form a star design on the peanut butter. (Birds love peanut butter, especially in winter.)

- Apples: Put toothpicks on all sides of apple (porcupine style). On the tip of each pick, place a raisin or cranberry.

- Tips on attracting birds to your tree: Put sunflower seeds or bird seed on ground around tree or in aluminum pie pan at base of tree, but out where it can be seen by birds. Especially after a fresh snowfall, put seeds around tree to help guide the birds to the treats you've provided. ❄

The Blessing of the Animals

PATRICIA SULLIVAN

My great-grandmother was born in a rural area of Ireland. She told me that during the great potato famine, no matter how poor her parents and their neighbors were, they always put out "a wee bit for the beasties" on Christmas Eve. This gift—this blessing—was given to the animals in honor of the role they played in the humble stable in Bethlehem.

So when we moved from the city to a farm in Wisconsin, my husband and I and our nine children decided to revive this family tradition.

At midnight, on Christmas Eve, we all troop down to the barn, through deep snow that crunches underfoot, and bring our gifts to the animals. We check to see that each animal has fresh water and clean bedding. Then the children take turns giving the horses and colts apples, carrots, oats and hay. The pigs are given extra mash and chopped vegetables. The cats and kittens, who have been playing around our feet, lap up big bowls of warm, frothy milk before getting little bags of catnip the girls have tied up in bundles for them. Our Irish setters Erin, Big Red and Old Mike wait patiently for their treat of meat broth and scraps over dry dog food.

"You are a good and faithful friend," says our youngest daughter Patti to each animal in turn, petting it fondly. "We ask the blessing of the animals, in Jesus' name."

When all the animals are fed and comfortable, we trudge back to our own snug home. The air is cold. The stars are bright. The night is silent. It is then that the holiness of Bethlehem's stable becomes very real to me. Our family sleeps then, I think, in heavenly peace. ❄